Detached

Surviving
Reactive Attachment Disorder

A personal story

Jessie Hogsett

Disclaimer

This book tells the story of my life with Reactive Attachment Disorder. Neither the author nor the publisher is engaged in rendering medical, psychiatric, or any other professional services by publishing this book. If any such assistance is required, the services of a qualified professional should be sought. The author and publisher will not be responsible for any liability, loss or risk incurred as a result of the use or application of any of the information contained in this book. Some names have been changed to protect the privacy of the people involved.

Acknowledgments

I'd like to thank my wife and children who have stuck by me every step of the way. I am grateful to those who have made a positive impact in my life. Most of all, I'd like to say thank you to my parents, Jerry and Suzanne Hogsett, who, above all, guided me in the right direction. They made difficult but necessary decisions to ensure that I'd grow up to be successful. They never gave up on me or my future. I love all of you.

ISBN 978-0-615-52279-1

JH Publishing   Modesto, California USA

Contents

Foreword

I may not have had the worst childhood ever. For whatever we feel is the worst, there is always someone else who has had a more difficult and painful life than we could imagine. However, things that I have gone through, things that I have experienced, even things that were out of my control, I have learned to overcome and integrate into my everyday life.

I know there are children, teens, mothers, fathers, teachers, counselors, social workers and many others who will be able to relate to the story I'm going to tell, and connect with what I'm going to say. I can only wish that my personal story offers hope, and a realization that some day we can all overcome even severe hardships in life, even those that made us feel as if the world had ended and that there was no hope left.

What Is Reactive Attachment Disorder?

Reactive Attachment Disorder (RAD), also sometimes called Attachment Disorder or Developmental Trauma Disorder, is a serious mental health condition in which infants and young children don't establish healthy bonds to parents or caregivers. Children with reactive attachment disorder typically were neglected or abused in infancy. They may have passed through many foster homes or lived in orphanages where their emotional needs weren't met.

Attachment disorders result from negative experiences in childrens' early relationships. If they feel repeatedly abandoned, isolated, power-less, or uncared-for, for whatever reason, they will learn that they can't depend on other people. They will feel that the world is a dangerous, frightening place. They will be unable to trust.

Because their basic needs for safety, comfort, affection, attention, nurturing and mental stimulation weren't met, these infants and young children didn't learn how to have loving and caring attachments to other people. They did not form a bond with their mother or anyone else. They grew up unable to give or receive affection because affection was foreign to them. They often grow up with feelings of anger, even rage, but have no idea whatsoever how to express them. Their only memory of any physical contact with their mothers or other caregivers might be that of being spanked, hit or beaten.

Often these children store up their unexpressed anger. The anger may then be expressed in a variety of negative ways such as destroying things, harming themselves or other people, stealing and lying.

Children with Reactive Attachment Disorder do not understand simple cause and effect. If they steal they cannot see how that would affect someone else. If they lie they most often believe what they are saying. When they get so upset they go into a rage, everything around them becomes a blur, "tunnel vision." They see only what is right in front of them and nothing else.

Because they haven't bonded with their mother or another caregiver, they feel no closeness to anyone. Because of this, they don't develop empathy. Without empathy they have no idea that anything they do has any effect on anyone else. They don't realize that their actions hurt other people. And if you tell them, they will not care.

They have no concept of their actions having consequences. They cannot attach to other people's feelings. This is why, more often than not, the same behaviors are exhibited, even after punishments are handed out. They just don't get it. They are unable to accept responsibility for anything they do. The RAD child seems uncaring and totally self-focused.

Both the diagnosis and treatment of RAD are difficult, and parents and caregivers are most often perplexed as they try to cope with the disorder. Despite exhibiting all the symptoms of RAD, and despite countless childhood visits with, and evaluation by, a wide range of medical professionals, no one knew I had RAD until I was 12 years old. And of all people, it was my adoptive mother Suzanne who discovered it. She happened upon a TV show that showcased an expert on RAD. She then followed up with in-depth reading, phoning and questioning. My RAD was later confirmed by psychologists and social workers.

RAD is a lifelong disorder, but with the right treatment and early interventions RAD children can grow up to become successful adults who function normally. RAD children can learn to develop healthy, lifelong, meaningful, trusting relationships with adults and others around them. They can grow up to be happy.

Part One

In the beginning — detachment

1 First memories

In February 1980 I was born as an underweight premature baby boy to a single alcoholic mother. She named me Jessie Fields Romine. Although my mother and father had split up by that time, I was still given my father's family name. In 1980 my birthplace, Modesto, California, was a sleepy agricultural town. My mother Leanne was a 23-year-old single mother struggling to make ends meet. She used drugs and alcohol while pregnant with me, and as a result, my heart stopped when I was born. I was lucky to have been born in a hospital where attentive doctors were able to restart my heart and save my life.

Also, as a result of my mother's drinking, I was born with fetal alcohol syndrome and hydrocephalus[1]. My hydrocephalus was detected by an ultrasound conducted on my mother while she was still pregnant. So soon after I was born, at about three months old, doctors placed a shunt[2] in my head. The surgery was a success. However, the doctors did not know what kind of life I'd have or even if I'd live to be an adult. But one thing was sure. I was alive. I had made it and was ready to get on with my new life.

My first memory goes back to when I was three years old. I remember going to a Bob's Big Boy restaurant to see my mother, who worked there

---

1. Hydrocephalus roughly translates to "water on the brain." The "water" refers to the Cerebral Spinal Fluid (CSF) that is produced in the brain. This fluid lubricates the brain and flows through the ventricles of the brain, lubricates the spinal cord and is absorbed into the spine. Hydrocephalus occurs when the flow of CSF becomes blocked and accumulates in the brain because it has nowhere to flow. As fluid builds the head starts to expand. Headaches, epileptic seizures, slurred speech, unsteady walking, poor balance, and many other afflictions can result.

2. A shunt is a long plastic tube inserted into the brain through the skull. A small burr hole is made in the skull and the tube is inserted through that. Mine was inserted into the fourth ventricle of my brain. The tube then ran out of the burr hole in my skull and directly under my skin, following a path on the right side of my body and ending in the peritoneal cavity. This is the cavity below the rib cage where the stomach, liver, and other organs are located. The fluid is then absorbed by the body and eliminated normally. The shunt carries away extra CSF and prevents a further build-up of fluid and the complications it could cause.

as a waitress. Doug, my mother's boyfriend at the time, took me there to eat lunch with her. I remember the huge Big Boy statue in front of the restaurant. It amazed me.

When we arrived, we were shown to a table by another worker. Shortly afterwards my mother came and sat down with us. I remember she always wore a pink waitress uniform with a white waist apron where she kept her pens. When she sat down I gave her a big hug and a kiss and I asked her, "Mommy, am I still three years old?" "Yes, Sweetie," she said, and she gave me a hug and a kiss. We ate shortly after that and then left. Mom would not be home for another few hours.

My mother and I lived in Ceres, near Modesto, in an upstairs apartment with my four-and-a-half-year-old sister Julia. There was a pool in the center of the apartment complex and an identical set of apartments on the other side of the pool. There was a wood fence with two sets of gates you had to go through to get to the apartments from the main road where the cars were parked.

From what I remember, Ceres was not a highly populated town. At least I don't remember seeing a lot of people. I saw lots of empty land with garbage strewn all over the ground and shopping carts left on sidewalks. My sister and I used those shopping carts as race cars and make-believe toys to ride around the street in. Usually I was in the cart and my sister pushed it. Since my mother was poor, she could not afford to buy us toys. We had to use our imaginations to entertain ourselves. The neighbors brought us toys their kids had outgrown, but we broke them in a matter of days.

I also remember a long staircase that went from our second floor apartment down to the ground floor where our mailbox was. Often when the mailman came he left a box of chocolate cookies for my sister and me at the bottom of the staircase. The problem was that there was only one box, so Julia and I raced downstairs to see who could get to the cookies first. Needless to say, I fell down those stairs quite often. But I got the cookies most of the time, and boy were they good. And sharing them with Julia was not in the plan. But few memories were good ones like this one. All in all, there were more bad memories than good ones.

2 Neglect

My sister Julia went to a preschool down the road from the apartment. I could see the school when I looked out the apartment window. I frequently ran from the apartment complex to go look for her at the school. Mom never really watched us that much.

Just imagine yourself as a three-year-old child left alone. You get up in the middle of the night and search your apartment for your mother because you just had a bad dream. You look everywhere, only to find she is not there. You wake up your sister and frantically search your entire place but Mom is nowhere to be found. Suddenly another feeling comes over you — panic, fear. What happened? Where is Mom? You start to cry, then you start to scream because you realize you are all alone and you are terrified. Where is she? Is she coming back? You look in her bedroom again but see she still isn't there. You go back to the bathroom and she still isn't there either.

More panic sets in. You start to wonder if she's coming back at all. You go to the living room and kitchen, frantically calling for her as your tears start flowing. When you realize that she is nowhere to be found, you run into your bedroom, climb up on your bed, curl up like a baby and rock back and forth, frightened and crying.

This was my young life in a nutshell. This and similar episodes happened repeatedly to my sister and me. Little did I know that things would get much much worse. I still think about those nights, wondering why we were left alone to fend for ourselves. I still don't have any answers.

When we think of abuse, the first thing that comes to most people's minds is physical abuse — beatings, bruising, cuts, burns, broken bones. As children, my sister and I experienced much of this. Another form of abuse is sexual abuse — being forced into sex acts including rape, kissing, fondling, talking about sexually explicit subjects, being forced to watch movies or shows with sexual content, and being touched in places where you're not supposed to be touched.

Then there is emotional abuse. This often happens without the perpetrators even realizing they are doing it. This includes name calling, verbally putting someone down, constantly dismissing them as if they don't exist, yelling, causing the child to cry so the caregiver feels more powerful, making promises and not following through with them, and telling the child everything they do is wrong and not good enough.

Neglect occurs when the caregivers fail to provide for the basic needs of the child in their care. This includes providing food, clothes, a clean and safe place to live, protection from harm, education, medical care, emotional support and love. It also includes being there to comfort the child in times of need. These forms of neglect all came into play in a big way in my and my sister's lives, and all by the time I was five years old.

Being left alone at night with my sister, without someone to protect us, was like being trapped in a nightmare that I couldn't wake up from. Fear, panic, anxiety and out-of-control feelings of desperation set in. We had to learn to fend for ourselves and cope with whatever was happening to us. We had to learn to figure out ways of dealing with things all by ourselves. I remember, for example, sitting in the bathtub with Julia. We got baths but we were put in there to wash ourselves.

At the same time we were normal curious kids, so of course we managed to get into things that we were not supposed to. Sometimes we were taken to our downstairs neighbors to stay with during the day while Mom was at work. But we were left alone at night. Where Mom went we never knew. She loved to go play bingo, hang out with neighbors, or go out on dates with her boyfriend. Sometimes she had one boyfriend, sometimes many. We had to take care of ourselves if Mom wasn't there, including finding something to eat and drink. We'd try to make meals from what we'd find — usually bread, bologna, and mustard, with water to drink. There was also spaghetti, our favorite, which we tried to cook. We got into things because no one was there to watch us. We made big messes in the kitchen. When Mom came home we always got punished when she saw the huge messes we made. Mom seemed to expect us to behave just like grownups, which of course didn't happen. We were only three and four years old. So then the punishments came, sometimes from Mom, but more often from her boyfriends.

We stayed up late since Mom wasn't ever there to tuck us into bed or read us a bedtime story. When she left us alone we pretty much did whatever we wanted. When Mom came home my sister and I were separated and locked in rooms for hours at a time. I was sent to the room my sister and I shared. My sister was locked in Mom's room. I could hear my sister's cries coming from the other room. They sounded like low sobs that seemed to be muffled by an object like a pillow. I wanted so badly to go hug Julia but I knew it would only cause more punishment for me and possibly for her too. The worst was that I never knew exactly what we had done that was so bad.

Then there was the belt. We were both whipped on our bare bottoms by one of Mom's boyfriends with his thick leather belt. The sting of the leather on my soft baby-like skin was like nothing I had ever felt before. My sister and I screamed in terrible pain, but screaming only made it worse. The more we cried out the more we got whipped. We learned really quickly how to go numb so we no longer felt the pain inflicted by the belt. After being whipped so many times our skin and nerves started to go numb. The welts made by the lashes prevented us from sitting down for a long time. I learned how to cope with the pain by laying flat on the floor on my stomach, then rocking my hips from side to side.

Then one day when I was with my sister she apparently did something really bad. I never knew what. She was hurled against the wall by one of Mom's boyfriends, spraining her leg and breaking her arm. Mom was there when these things went on but she stayed in the background. Since she was an alcoholic, she may even have been drunk most of the time and not totally aware of what was happening to us. Or maybe she was too intimidated by the boyfriend who was perpetrating the abuse at the time. Maybe she was afraid the boyfriend might hurt her too if she said anything. Perhaps she felt helpless, unable to intervene, unable to do anything about it. Maybe she felt totally powerless. Whatever her excuse might have been, my mom was there, but she did nothing.

Mom had some nice boyfriends too. They weren't all mean. But the ones that were mean I felt terrorized by. Once I smacked my mom, thinking that would get her attention. It didn't. She just smacked me back.

Although Mom hugged and kissed me on rare occasions, I still felt distant from her. I did not feel loved by her. I did not feel she really cared about me. Maybe it was because I was left alone so much. Maybe it was because I lived in constant fear. Maybe it was because her show of affection felt superficial. It surely didn't seem to come from the heart.

I longed for her to hold me, to hold me tightly, to draw me towards her and wrap her arms around me and never let go. I needed her to caress me, to cover me with kisses that showed I meant the world to her. But the only signs of affection I got were quick superficial hugs and insincere kisses on the cheek. She was just going through the motions of what she thought a mother should do. Maybe she was just trying to get through yet another day of her difficult life.

She called me, "Sweetie," then left me alone all night to call her name for hours to no avail. She was physically and emotionally distant. In fact, she was more than that. She was physically and emotionally unavailable. She was absent. She was gone.

I don't remember ever being praised by her, ever being given positive feedback, ever feeling I was a good child, a worthy child, a child worth anything. It all confused me and made me not trust her. She said one thing and did something else. She kissed and hugged me but I felt totally disconnected from her. I felt no bond with her whatsoever. I was detached.

My life wasn't always horrible. There were some good times too, but these were few and far between. I remember playing wiffle ball in the park with my mom and on several occasions we went camping and fishing. Sometimes the fishing trips were just afternoon outings, but the times I liked the best were the overnight camping and fishing trips. I loved to fish because it was so peaceful and because I always caught more fish than anyone else. Most importantly, I got to spend some time with Leanne. These rare moments made me so happy.

My mom's brother, Uncle Danny, joined us on some of the trips. He was a great guy. He had long hair and a mustache. He carried around a small axe for chopping firewood if we needed some. He was a true outdoorsman and someone I looked up to, someone who paid attention to me. He took me on several fishing trips and taught me a lot about fishing. I craved any attention I could get and cherished this time with him.

By the time I turned four we had moved out of the apartment and also in and out of several other places. It was not unusual for my sister and me to sleep in our family car because Mom did not have anywhere for us to live. Even though Mom lived with us in the car, it was still scary, cramped, and uncomfortable. Julia and I curled up in the back seat together. We were also miserably cold. We were homeless much of the time, although we seemed to stay more in apartments that in the car. Even though Mom always seemed to have a job, she couldn't always afford an apartment. It was not unusual for us to wear the same clothes for a week or two at a time because Mom didn't seem to wash them. It was not unusual for much of anything to happen then. This life was what we thought was normal.

I started to be openly angry, even defiant. When I got in trouble I screamed and yelled at the top of my lungs. When Mom tried to calm me down, sometimes I slapped her in the face. Sometimes she slapped me back. My sister was not off limits for me either. I grabbed anything she had out that she was playing with. I either tore it apart or hid it from her. Doing this made her so mad. I loved her, but for some reason it made me feel good to do these things. I felt like I was in control. I felt maybe I wasn't completely powerless, completely helpless after all. I was starting to become aggressive and I reveled in it!

Then one day we went to a woman's house. She was referred to as "Grandma," but I don't know if she really was my grandmother or not.

I couldn't wait until we got there. I was so excited. A red tricycle was there for us and all kinds of toys to play with. Mom needed a break and I needed some fun! Grandma's house seemed to be the perfect place to be. I remember it had carpeted floors, couches and matching furniture. Sweet smells floated through the air, smells of different spices, flowers, and perfume. It was neat and tidy. It felt safe and warm and cozy. Grandma was happy to see my sister and me and we felt welcome there. I went straight for the toys. Mom said, "Goodbye," but I paid no attention. I just wanted to ride my tricycle. When Mom dropped us off at Grandma's house, she usually came back in a day or so to get us.

On the surface Grandma's house seemed perfect. But it was far from perfect. As soon as Mom left a different scene unfolded. I was not prepared for what was going to happen while staying there. I was now four years old. What on earth did I know about cleaning a bathtub? Apparently Grandma thought that Julia and I should know because one morning we were made to do it. I didn't know what I was doing of course. As a result, when Grandma came to check on my progress, she saw that I wasn't doing a very good job. As I leaned over the tub to scour a spot inside it, she grabbed my head in her two strong hands and squished it against the side of the bathtub with all her might. She used her hands as you'd squish a piece of modeling clay in your hands. She yelled a few mean words, then made me sit on a stool watching as my sister was made to finish the cleaning.

My head hurt really badly and I thought my face was bleeding. But all I found dripping from me were just the tears flowing down my cheeks. I felt like throwing up. All I wanted to do was lie down, but I was not allowed to until the cleaning was finished. After this incident Grandma apologized. But all I recall is me telling her I was sorry for not doing it right and that I'd do better next time. I couldn't wait for my mom to come get me. Even after all the things Mom did to me, I still needed her. I missed her and was happy when she came to pick us up.

Many more things happened to me, both good and bad, with my mom and her many boyfriends, but I can't remember them well. Some people say that when bad things happen to you, you can block them out. Maybe that is what I did. I don't know. All I know is that, at that time, our normal lives would have been considered hellish by others. Even when we had a place to live, we lived in filth. Food and dirt were all over some of the walls and on the kitchen counters. Dishes filled the sink. I remember walking on the carpet and feeling something sticky and gross under my feet. There was always a dirt ring in the bathtub and all kinds of splattered food in the refrigerator and freezer. That was life in my eyes.

By now I was getting really bad headaches, bad enough to make me cry. I cried so much that it drove my mom crazy. She yelled at me out of frustration because she tried to figure out what was wrong with me and could not. Many times she just left me alone to cry because she could not stand the noise, and she couldn't deal with the frustration of not knowing what to do. She couldn't make my headaches go away, and she couldn't stop my crying.

She finally took me to the hospital emergency room and it was there that she found out what was wrong with me. The shunt which was supposed to keep my hydrocephalus in check was not working properly. I was going to need another surgery. With hydrocephalus there was always the concern that I'd need shunt replacements, as shunts are not guaranteed to last forever. They can break, leak, get blocked, or an infection can set in.

The emergency room doctors performed a CT scan. I had to lie down on a table and the scanner was placed over my head. It took pictures of my whole head. I had to lie very still, which was hard for me. I was only four years old and my head was still hurting really badly. The doctors noticed that my shunt had an infection around it and that it was not functioning properly. They said that I'd need to have it replaced right away.

That night they admitted me to the hospital. The doctor was a very friendly, easy-going guy. I felt comfortable around him. He showed me the razor he was going to use to shave the back of my head in order to do the surgery. Then he blew into a latex glove, made a balloon hand and drew a smiley face on it. After he shaved the back of my head he put a blue hair net on my head, blue foot covers on my feet and wheeled me to the surgery room. Mom was waiting outside. As I was wheeled to the operating room she gave me a big kiss and told me everything was going to be all right.

The surgeons replaced the shunt catheter inside my brain and put new tubing which ran from my head to my abdominal cavity. I woke up in a bed in the hospital pediatric unit. I felt very tired. I had a big bandage on my head and an IV in my arm. My mom came in, said everything had gone well and that she was glad to see me. She told me she had been so worried. I was glad it was all over. But this would not be the last time I'd have to deal with this issue. I'd have constant unrelenting headaches for many years to come.

Part Two

New places, new faces — fear and loathing

3 One-way journey

My sister and I soon found out that we were about to embark upon a journey that would become the hardest part of our lives. I was now four and a half years old. My sister was five and a half. Mom told us we were going for a drive, but she didn't tell us where we were going. Mom didn't tell us much. Maybe we were moving again. After all, moving happened a lot. But there were no suitcases in the car. We'd brought nothing with us. Maybe we were going to the park. It was fun to go to the park and play. But Mom was crying in the front seat of the car. Why?

My sister was listening to her yellow tape player in the back seat. She didn't seem to care where we were going. Maybe she knew and had just forgotten to tell me. I sat in the back seat next to her. I looked back at our apartment as we drove away, not realizing that it would be the last time I'd ever see it. I also didn't know it would be the last time we would ever live with Mom. We drove for what seemed like an eternity. It was probably only an hour or so, but to a child of four, the ride seemed to go on forever.

We drove up to a big building. It looked like a doctor's office building. There were a few windows in front and two doors. I was sure I was going to get a checkup now. Maybe something was wrong with my newest surgery. I remember my mom unstrapping me from my car seat and taking my sister and me inside. She was still crying. I still did not know why. There had been nothing but silence in the car.

The inside of the building was even bigger than what it seemed like on the outside. There was a big desk as soon as you walked in. To the right and left were long walkways that met each other on the other side and formed a circle. Along the edge of the walls of the circle were several doors. I remember seeing other kids and grownups coming out those doors. Some couches, benches, a few TVs, and the coolest thing, a pool table, were in the center of the circle.

My mom told my sister and me to go sit down on the couches while she talked to the lady at the desk in the front. I ran to the pool table and began to hit the balls with the other balls on the table. I wasn't sure how to play so I made up my own rules and played my own game. My sister sat at a nearby table, still listening to her yellow tape player.

I glanced over at my mom. She was still crying. Every once in a while she looked over at us. Finally she called us over. I wondered what she was going to say. I excitedly ran over to her. She got down on her knees and looked me straight in the eye. I will never forget what she said: "Mommy loves you and I want the best for you. You are going to go to a better place where you can get the love and care that you both deserve." She gave both of us a big hug and a kiss. I started crying. So did Julia. We both yelled out, "Mommy don't go!" Besides that, I said nothing.

A few grownups came over and held us forcibly while my mom left the building. I tried desperately to get free so I could run after her, but I could not break free. My mom was leaving me. I was trapped. I was powerless. No one would listen to me. No one would help me. I must have cried until I could not cry any more, until there were no more tears left. I felt empty, rejected, unwanted, thrown away.

That would be the last time we would see her for a long time. I was then told that the place we were in was a children's shelter in San Jose, California. My sister was still crying. I remember hugging her and telling her it would all be OK and that Mom would be coming back. Maybe I thought this because I was used to the whims of our mom. But I was now unsure of everything. I soon felt very angry and very scared. I felt alone again. Uncertainty set in. I started to wonder what we had done wrong. What had we done that was so terrible that our own mother would just walk out on us like that? There had been no warning, nothing. Was this our punishment?

I had so many questions but no answers. Most of all I wondered what was going to happen to us next. I did not understand what Mom meant by "going to a better place." I wanted to stay with her. I did not want to go anywhere else. What on earth was so wrong with me that my own mother would just leave me? What was so terrible about me that caused me to find myself in such a strange new place, surrounded by people I did not know?

Just then I heard a voice, "Hello, my name is Maureen and you are going to be staying with me." There was a woman standing a few feet in front of me. She was of average height, had blond curly hair that fell to her shoulders, and was a bit fat. She looked like she was wearing makeup. She did not smile.

My sister and I got into Maureen's van and we started to drive off. Julia was still crying and as I looked back at the shelter I could not help but feel lost and lonely. I turned back around and started to cry. I must have cried myself to sleep because the next thing I remember was the van pulling up in front of a two-story house.

Another new place and another new adventure were about to unfold. I stayed close to my sister that day, as she was all I had left. Mom was gone, at least for now, and I was sure not going to let my sister go too. I was not going to lose the last person in my life who made me feel safe. I just hoped my mom would come back and take us back. I was hoping that, like in the past, she would be gone for a day or so and then would be back.

Maureen's was a temporary foster home. Kids unable to stay in their own homes due to their parents' inability to care for them could go there and get proper care and attention. From places like Maureen's kids went to longer term foster homes or became available for adoption. Before a child could be made available for adoption his or her parents had the opportunity to get the child back. They had to prove they could provide security, comfort, attention, food and a stable place to live. The State of California gave them 18 months to prove this. Most of the time this did not happen.

The parents had to attend regular court hearings where their progress in meeting these standards was judged. If, at the end of the 18 months, these requirements were not met, the parents' rights were terminated and the child was made available for adoption. A child could also become available for adoption if both parents agreed to sign away their legal rights. If they didn't, the court could terminate the parents' rights after the 18 month time limit was over.

The adoption was final when the family who wanted to adopt and the child who was to be adopted went to court and signed the necessary paperwork to finalize the adoption. At this point all of the child's documentation was usually changed to reflect the adoption. The birth certificate was changed to reflect the new family's name, with the adoptive parents' names replacing the names of the birth parents. The child's Social Security card was changed to reflect the new last name, etc. The original documents prior to adoption were sealed. When a child wasn't yet free for adoption he went into the foster care system. While in a foster home the child could be visited by his parents if the court granted them visitation rights.

I remember seeing buckets of toys in Maureen's living room and a big play mat in the center of the room. I thought maybe being there was not going to be too bad after all. There were other kids to play with, plenty of toys, and I felt safe.

Sure, I got into some trouble when I was there. That was to be expected. I was only five. My sister and I slept in separate rooms, she in the girls' room and I in the boys' room. There were six or seven kids at Maureen's at the time. There were two boys to a room. I had the top bunk and when I could not fall asleep I always picked at the popcorn ceiling. When we got into trouble we were made to sleep in the garage, which had been made into another bedroom. It had a bed, carpet, and a dresser but not much else. There was only room for one child in there. I spent two or three nights sleeping in that place, two or three nights that seemed like a nightmare.

It hurt deep inside to know I was being punished like that by Maureen. I thought that this was supposed to be a safe place and a caring place like my mom had said. So why was I being punished? My impression of Maureen was a bad one. She was not the type of person who filled me with either comfort or joy. I tried to steer clear of her when I could. To me she was just plain mean and I wanted to go home. I wanted more than anything to be back with my mom. I thought about Mom every minute of every day.

The food was mostly inedible and I always left the table hungry. It was not that there was not enough food. I just didn't eat much because I did not like the food that was served. I ate some things because I was made to eat what was in front of me and, if I did not, I was sent to bed without eating. So I ate the minimal amount and soon dreaded mealtimes.

I was still not potty trained. I had frequent accidents and that upset Maureen too. She yelled at me in disgust, wanting to know how I could poo in my pants like that. She did not understand. I did not understand why I did that either. I felt really hurt and helpless when that happened. I was then made to get in the bathtub while her daughter washed me. I think her daughter was in her early twenties or maybe a little younger. I did not want her looking at me. Above all, I didn't want her touching me. All the mistreatment just fueled my anger, making me want to just shut my feelings down, turn them off. I was never toilet trained by Mom so I didn't know a darn thing I could do about the "accidents" I had. Why couldn't Maureen and her daughter just leave me alone?

Just then a big event was about to make a huge change in my life. I did not know it then, but I'd soon meet a couple who would later become my adoptive parents, my permanent family. They were Jerry and Suzanne Hogsett. One afternoon they came to Maureen's. I think that I had been there for a few weeks by then. I don't remember the Hogsetts coming in, but I remember Maureen leading me into a big room on the right when you first come in the front door. There they were. The man, Jerry, was tall, at least to me. He had blond hair, a long blond beard and a mustache. He was wearing nice clothes and smiled at me when he first saw me.

The woman with him, Suzanne, was a little shorter than he was, but she still seemed tall to me. She also had a big smile on her face when I came in. They introduced themselves to me. What I remember best is that they got down on my level, on their knees, so they'd be at eye level with me. That made me feel comfortable and at ease. We played a card game or two, which I won because I cheated big time. We talked for a while about what things I liked and disliked. We talked about my favorite food, tacos, and we laughed a lot. I felt at home with them, but I still didn't know why they were there. I had people coming in and out of my life all the time, so this was quite normal.

I wondered why my sister was not there with me in the room with these people. When the Hogsetts left I gave them a hug, and, oddly enough, I felt a sense of calm and well being after meeting them. Up to that point, no one had made me feel wanted like the Hogsetts did in the short time we had spent together. It had been a good day. I had made two new friends — people who seemed to listen to me and who seemed to care.

My sister ended up leaving Maureen's before I did. No one at Maureen's ever told us much of anything. One day I didn't see my sister and I wondered where she was. I then found out she was gone. Gone! The day she left was a huge loss for me. The one person I was close to and looked up to, the only person beside Mom I cared about, was no longer there to console me. My feelings of uncertainty and being alone set in all over again. I cried and cried and wasn't sure if and when I'd ever see her again. She had abandoned me too.

My mom had dumped me and now my sister was gone too. I don't remember my sister even telling me goodbye. She was just gone. Her clothes were gone. Her toys were gone. Her big grin was gone. Nothing in that house was left to remind me of her. My young five year old life was falling apart and there was nothing whatsoever I could do about it.

My sister now became everything to me. I felt so terribly alone. The pain of loss enveloped me. It would not stop. I'd find out many years later that my adoptive parents, the Hogsetts, wanted to adopt my sister and me together. But they were not allowed to. Julia and I had different fathers and no one could find my biological father in order to get him to sign away his rights to me. Social Services finally found him in an Arkansas prison, where he'd been serving time for drugs, and he signed his rights away. Julia had been available for adoption before going to Maureen's and I hadn't, so we couldn't be adopted together.

Because my biological father was half Cherokee Indian, that made me one-quarter Cherokee Indian. That fact was another obstacle to my being adoptable right away. Social Services had to get permission from the Cherokee Council for me to be adopted. By the Cherokee standard I had just enough Native American blood that I could have been sent to a reservation to live. So needless to say, there were many hurdles that had to be jumped in order for my new parents to adopt me.

When Jerry and Suzanne signed up and qualified as foster parents, they had no intention of adopting a child, any child. But once I came to live with them and they fell in love with me, all that changed. They told me they'd chosen me as their foster child because they thought I was the smartest kid of all those available, and also the cutest. Later, my mom Leanne decided she didn't want to bother trying to prove she was a fit parent, so she signed her rights away, making me available for adoption. Then Jerry and Suzanne applied to Social Services and were approved as adoptive parents.

My mom Leanne liked the Hogsetts and felt I'd be given the proper care and love and I'd have a stable environment. She also knew they'd let her come visit me and keep in touch with me.

But, at the time, I saw this move as my mother giving up on me. I saw this as her not caring about me or wanting me any more. This made me very upset and made me feel more and more abandoned. It felt like I was being thrown away, this time for good.

I stayed at Maureen's for another week before the Hogsetts came to take me home with them. At first I was a foster child of the Hogsetts. I was five years old then and would be their foster child for another two years while the issues with finding my biological father and with the Cherokee Council were resolved.

I remember clearly the day I arrived at the Hogsetts' home in Palo Alto, about 30 miles south of San Francisco. Their house was a single story gray wood and glass Eichler home with a fence and gate in front. There was a driveway and a small front yard outlined by juniper bushes. As you walked through the gate, there was a big patio with patio furniture and a brick barbeque. To the left was a door that led to the garage. On the right side of the house was a walkway that went around to the backyard. The front door was straight ahead.

I was very anxious and scared about going into that house. I was already used to living in different places a lot, but I still couldn't help but feel nervous and frightened. After all, this was another new place and I was unsure what to expect. I missed my mom and sister terribly. I thought about them all the time, almost every waking moment. I desperately wanted to be with them both. I wanted my sister in this new house with me. She was the closest person I had. I wanted to hug her and hold her hand. I wanted to hear her tell me that everything was going to be OK. But when I looked around I was reminded that I was alone on this journey. There was no sister or mother here, only an unfamiliar house in an unfamiliar town.

As I went into the house it was very quiet. I was not used to this. I was used to people coming in and out and being around all the time. I became more nervous. On the drive to the house Suzanne had said she had a friend for me to meet when we got home. I wondered what she was talking about. Was there going to be someone coming to say, "Hi"? Were there other children in the house? I crossed the threshold and waited just inside the front door, expecting someone to run down the hallway to greet me. I imagined seeing my sister come running down the hall, happy and excited, and wrapping her arms around me. I imagined other kids, perhaps a boy, running down that hall.

But no one came. There were no children laughing. There were no children playing. In fact, there were no children at all. No children came.

There were just Jerry and Suzanne. When I met them at Maureen's I felt very comfortable with them. But now, what was going on began to sink in. I was in a strange house with people I had only met once. What did this mean? Why was I there? Where was my sister? Where was my mother? My trepidation turned to disappointment, then despair. I was a child alone. All alone. Clearly this was not a place for me.

Suzanne led me down the hall to a room where I found out what she meant by "a friend." In the room were a dresser, a closet, toys all over the place, and a bed. On the bed were all kinds of stuffed animals. Were those the friends Suzanne was talking about? I looked around at everything in the room, trying to make sense of it all. I had never had all these things before. I did not even realize at first that those things were even mine, or that I'd even be allowed to play with them. I was hesitant to touch anything, but I was assured that it was OK and that in fact the toys and stuffed animals were mine to keep. This was my room.

Toots the cat also lived with us. She had long grey fur with a fuzzy white belly. She was somewhat shy. Suzanne told me that she was the friend she was talking about. When I saw her I reached down to pet her, but she ran away to hide somewhere. Suzanne assured me that it was only because she did not know me and that in time she would take to me. I had a special place for animals in my heart. I don't know why, but when I saw cats or dogs or any other tame animal, it calmed me. It was an instant connection. It was as if I could relate to the sad eyes an animal often looks at you with. It was as if I could sense that the animal was not a threat and that it offered comfort. After seeing what was in my room I was given a tour of the rest of the house. Jerry and Suzanne's room was right next to mine. It was reassuring to know that if I needed help or was scared, that they were right next door.

They had a good sized backyard with a few fruit trees. Hidden beneath some big tree branches was a big round thing. I wondered what it was. I came to find out it was called a hot tub. I had never seen one before. The living room was separated from the dining room and kitchen by a wall that went from the floor a third of the way up to the ceiling. There were doors leading to the backyard through the living room, through Jerry and Suzanne's bedroom, and through my bedroom. All in all, it was a good sized place. It had four bedrooms, two bathrooms and a big open kitchen, dining, and living room area. I did not expect to stay there long. I just thought, as usual, that I'd be moving again soon.

I finished taking a tour of the house and put my few belongings away in my room. It was different having my own room. I had never had my own room before and now I did and it was lonely. I had very few clothes and was not sure where or when I'd be getting more. Everything I owned was in a paper bag I brought with me from Maureen's house. Everything I had, my whole life — memories, treasures, everything, fit into one brown paper grocery bag. Everything!

I did have one special toy in that bag, however. It was something I never went anywhere without, something I held close to me and seldom let go of. It was a small soft cloth doll that said, "I love you" across its chest. It was from my mom Leanne. I was unsure what love was. I snuggled with the doll, but not because it made me feel my mom loved me. I held it close to me because it was the only material thing I had that connected me to her, the only thing she'd ever given me that I was still able to hang on to, something that reminded me of her. Many nights I cried myself to sleep holding the doll next to me as I lay curled up like a baby.

I felt very nervous and uneasy in this new setting. I remember the Hogsetts repeatedly trying to make me feel at home, repeatedly asking me what I needed, what I wanted, repeatedly trying to hug and kiss me. But I still felt very lonely. I just wanted to get out of there.

This was still the first day. On that first night Jerry made the home-made tacos he'd promised to make when we met at Maureen's. They were the best — fresh vegetables, grated cheese, ground hamburger, big homemade taco shells. I had never had any meal like that before and I could hardly believe it. I was also given a big glass of milk to wash it down. I didn't know how to take it, but boy did I eat. Another new thing was that we ate at a table as a family. I was not used to that. I did not know how to act. I didn't even know that this was the normal thing that most people did. This was a new experience and a lot to take in.

After dinner was bath time. Suzanne drew the bath water for me. She did not put a lot of water in the tub, maybe six inches, and it wasn't too hot. I got in the tub and she sat in the bathroom while I took my bath. She even helped me wash my hair and body. I remember Jerry calling her while I was in the bathtub. She left and told me that she'd be right back.

All of a sudden that feeling of abandonment came back to me. I waited for her to come right back, but she didn't come right away. I started to yell her name at the top of my lungs. I was getting scared. I yelled and yelled and then started to cry. She came running down the hall, scooped me out of the tub, wrapped me in a towel, kissed me, hugged me, and said over and over again she was sorry.

She promised me that she'd never leave me alone in the bathtub again. We went to my room and she helped me get my pajamas on. Jerry came in a little while later and read me a bedtime story. This was another thing I was not used to. No one had ever read a story to me before. I lay there and listened and soon fell asleep. I woke up the next morning to find that I was still in the same place, in the same bed, with the same stuffed animals around me. Day one was over and I was still safe.

But then I felt something else. My sheets were wet. What happened? I realized I had wet the bed that night. I got frightened again. I was sure I was going to get spanked or hit with a belt because I wet the bed. That was what always happened in the past and that was what I expected. I took my underpants off and put them into my closet, hiding them under some other clothes. I quickly tried to cover the soaked sheets with my blanket, but then Jerry and Suzanne came in. I froze and started to cry. They asked what was wrong and I told them. I waited for the beating to start, but instead they said it was OK and that accidents happen.

They took me to the bathtub to get me cleaned up and Suzanne changed my sheets. I was confused again and not sure what to do. I relaxed a little, but at the same time I was still scared that I was going to be in trouble for wetting the bed. I'd learn over time the reasons why this happened. A lot of my bed-wetting had to do with my hydrocephalus, which made me pee frequently. It also made me need to go instantly. Sometimes I'd end up peeing in the grocery store or in other public places we happened to be. That was very embarrassing for me and I felt awful about it.

Jerry and Suzanne tried to toilet train me so I wouldn't soil my underpants and I wouldn't have accidents, especially in public. But that didn't seem to work. They thought my lack of control might be due to my medical problems, but my doctors didn't seem to think so. Some people even suggested I did these things so no one would want to be close to me, so I could stay detached. Over time I learned to overcome this and eventually stop the soiling, wetting my bed and peeing in public altogether.

As I've said, I was five years old when I came to live at the Hogsetts as a foster child. Shortly thereafter I was enrolled in public school, Palo Verde Elementary School in Palo Alto, California. I started my kinder-garten year there with my teacher Pam. She was a wonderful woman who was always patient and who always seemed to smile.

During this time my mom came to see me three or four times. We'd sit on the Hogsetts' patio and have a great visit. Sometimes she'd bring me presents. One time she brought a bunch of colorful balloons. During this period she told me that she'd be coming back for me when she was able to land a steady job and be able to rent a big place for us to stay. So for many years to come I always thought she'd be coming at any time to take me back with her. Jerry and Suzanne also thought Leanne was coming to take me back and that my stay was temporary. As such they both made work commitments for the future, for times they thought I'd no longer be with them.

Jerry worked for IBM as a computer software engineer in Palo Alto. A great project opportunity opened up for him at an IBM laboratory in England, so he was sent there for a two-year job assignment. Suzanne and I stayed behind because she was still working. She taught travel classes and led groups of Americans on tours around the U.S. and to different countries. Suzanne and I would be going to England later, a couple of months after Jerry arrived there.

Suzanne had to finish the work commitments she'd made before she and Jerry met me at Maureen's. Her traveling on job assignments meant a sitter had to come live in the house to take care of me while she was gone. She was usually gone for two weeks, back for a few months or so, then gone again. One time the sitter was Stan, a relative of Jerry's. I did not know Stan but I was assured that everything would be fine because Jerry said he was a great guy. Again, another person in my life. They seemed to come and go, come and go. After all, Jerry was gone and Suzanne seemed to be in and out a lot. So, in a sense, I was just going with the flow of things, as I had done many times before.

I still struggled with soiling my underpants. I do not remember exactly why, but I never seemed to make it to the toilet in time. Some people believe that kids with Reactive Attachment Disorder do these kinds of things in order to make people stay away from them. The more they smell, the less likely it is someone will want to be close to them. If no one gets close to them they don't risk getting attached to them. If they don't get attached they figure they won't get hurt again. As RAD kids have these major attachment issues, this makes sense to me.

One day when Stan was there we were getting ready to go spend the day in Berkeley. I was dressed and ready to go and then suddenly it happened. I soiled my underpants. But instead of telling Stan, I left my underpants on and acted like nothing happened. I was too scared to tell him. I didn't know this guy. In fact I wouldn't even have told Jerry or Suzanne. I was embarrassed, angry at the fact that I soiled my underwear, and unsure of what the punishment would be if I said anything. So I decided to keep it to myself.

Stan found out however because of the smell. He took me into the bathroom and told me to pull down my pants. When he saw what had happened he got very upset. He started yelling at me, asking me why I did not go to the bathroom in time and why I did not tell him. I did not know what to say. I didn't know why. I had no idea. And I didn't seem to be able to do anything whatsoever about it. All I could do in response to his question was to shrug my shoulders. Then I started to cry.

Stan ran a bath for me and set me in the tub. But he then grabbed the soiled underpants and plunked them right down on top of my head, making me wear them like a hat while I took a bath. At this point I was crying so hard I just wanted to get out of the tub and run away and never come back. Anger started to set in. I was furious. And for one moment I wanted to just jump out of the tub, take the underpants off my head, and whack Stan in his face with them. I wanted to hit him hard. But I did not. I did nothing. And I said nothing. I knew I was powerless.

Stan washed me and got me dressed. Later he apologized. He tried giving me a hug, but I pulled away. We did not go to Berkeley that day or any other day. We stayed home, quietly avoiding each other. I stayed in my room in my bed and wrapped myself up with all my stuffed animals. They made a barrier around me that I thought no one could get through. I felt protected by them. I felt they all had a soul and that they would shield me from harm. I lay there that night talking to them as if they were real animals that were able to hear what I was saying. I soon fell asleep.

Stan stayed for two weeks while Suzanne was away. She came home and we packed up and flew to England. Jerry had already taken Michael, his 13-year-old son from his previous marriage, with him to England. So we would be a family of four and I would finally have a brother.

4 Off to England

We flew to London on a British Airways 747 jumbo jet and we got to sit on the top deck of the plane in Business Class. I even got to take a tour of the cockpit. It was so cool. I loved it. For some part of the flight I stretched out and slept on the floor beneath the seats Suzanne and I had been assigned.

We lived in the south of England in the small village of Chandlers Ford, near Winchester. I attended Fryern Infant School for the remainder of my kindergarten year. It was there I learned to read. I was still a foster child so certain legal requirements had to be met in order for me to be able to leave the U.S. and live in England. English Social Services came to our house to make sure it was safe for me to live in. They said they wanted to make sure "there wasn't any coal stored in the bathtub." We lived happily in England for the next two years. Living there was quite an adventure. I had to adjust to a new way of living and culture. It was not long before I spoke with a distinct English accent. Jerry and Suzanne thought it was the cutest thing.

A woman named Dee was an English family friend who lived in our village. I don't recall why I stayed with her, but I did for quite a while. While I was there I stole things from her. These ranged from little items I thought were cool to candy she had laying around. I even managed to go through her purse and take money. Jerry and Suzanne found out and made me tell Dee what I'd done. I was frightened because I didn't know how she would react. She told me she was upset and that I wasn't allowed to come there any more. That really did not matter to me. I just had an urge to take things. It did not matter who I took them from or where I was.

It snowed a few times while we lived in southern England. I remember making a snowman in the backyard, which was a lot of fun. The double decker red school bus was my favorite though. I waited at the bus stop every morning, looking to see if the bus was coming. I always sat on the upper deck. There was a petite little girl who attended the same school and rode on the school bus with me. Her name was Louise. She was so pretty. Her eyes were big and blue and she had long flowing dark hair. She looked like a little doll. I had a childhood crush on her. I made sure that we sat together every day we rode the bus.

While living in England we took car and plane trips to many different European countries — Switzerland, France, Belgium, Italy, San Marino, the Netherlands, and Germany. We even visited Turkey. I was six years old at the time. I remember it snowing as we passed through Paris and Jerry driving all night to get us to someplace warm.

Now what six-year-old with a past like mine would get the chance to travel all over Europe? But I took it for granted. I'd much rather have been home in my room with my stuffed animals or playing with my friends. My home and the English village we lived in were safe havens for me. All the places we traveled to were different from anything I had ever known. We walked a lot in Europe and I hated it. My legs hurt badly, but when I complained to Jerry and Suzanne, I felt like they did not listen. Instead they made me feel I should be grateful to be able to see these places that not too many kids my age could visit. On several occasions I walked off so I didn't have to listen to them. I just wanted to run off and be on my own and not come back. I wanted to find someone who understood me.

Soon, while we were still overseas, I started cutting holes in my clothes because I was angry and frustrated. Every time I thought of having to walk for any distance, I cut my clothes. Every time I was dragged to see something I did not care to see, I cut holes in the clothes I was wearing. I also did this whenever Jerry and Suzanne got upset with me because I did not seem to be having a good time.

Destroying something let me release my anger. I also felt I gained control. I used anything sharp that would cut. The cuts started small but got bigger as my anger got more intense. I would run off and by the time Suzanne would finally catch up to me, I'd have cut at least ten holes in my pants. When asked why I did it, I'd just shrug my shoulders and say, "Because."

"Because" became my favorite expression. It was simple, easy, and seemed to sum up everything. I did not know at the time why I cut my clothes. I just wanted to. Boy did this irritate Jerry and Suzanne. But I did not care. I was fascinated with cutting things. Soon the cutting would lead to more serious issues.

I especially liked destroying things Suzanne had given me — clothes, games, toys, pictures, anything. In the back of my mind I always hoped that if I made her mad enough she'd go away and my real mom would come for me. I didn't destroy much of anything Jerry had given me because he was the only Dad I'd ever known.

It was also during this time that I started a new behavior. When Suzanne would come sit by me, I'd get up and run off. She'd try to kiss me, but when I saw this was about to happen, I'd just turn away. It seems I was hellbent to reject her. She was not my "real mom" and I did not want her. This behavior stemmed in part from my not learning more about love and affection when I was very young. I also didn't want to feel close to anyone again after my mom had left me.

I look back on those travel experiences now and kick myself. The trips were a once in a lifetime chance and I wish I'd enjoyed them more and really learned to appreciate different cultures. But at age six, and with the issues I was grappling with, I didn't know what appreciation was.

After two years in England, Jerry's overseas assignment with I.B.M. was over. On the way back to the United States we went on a trip around the world. I got to go on safari in Kenya and Tanzania and visit the island of Zanzibar. I got a neat haircut in Harare, Zimbabwe. I swam in beautiful warm water and stayed in a grass hut in Fiji. We saw koalas and kangaroos in Sydney, then went to Perth, Australia. We ended this trip on the island of St. Lucia in the Caribbean. I don't remember the exact order we saw these places in, but I do remember these highlights.

5 Young rebel

After our around-the-world trip, we arrived back home in Palo Alto. I was glad to be back. I just wondered when my mom was going to come get me to take me back with her. Now that we were back it would be easier for her to come get me. After all, now she didn't have to travel across the ocean to find me. Hopefully she'd come soon I thought to myself, as I missed her terribly. I assumed it would be a matter of hours, or maybe days, before she would come get me. Why wasn't she waiting for me at the airport when I got off the plane? Where was she?

My mom did phone and she spoke with me several times. She wanted to know how I was doing in school and how I was doing day to day. I really enjoyed those calls and looked forward to getting them. She even promised to come visit me at the Hogsetts. I got so excited! Mom was finally coming! Was this going to be the day she would pick me up and take me to live with her? Was this the day I had waited so long for? I could hardly contain my excitement. My mom was coming and that was all that mattered.

Jerry and Suzanne told me to calm down because I was very excited and hyper, but I didn't want to listen to them. They could not tell me what to do. Who were they to tell me what to do? My real mom was coming and that meant to me that I didn't have to listen to these other people any more. That meant I didn't need to do anything these other people told me to do. They weren't my real parents. The day went on, but Mom did not come. I kept looking out the kitchen window, anxiously waiting for her to open the gate, anxiously waiting to see her standing there. But that did not happen. Mom did not come.

I cried and cried and felt so angry and let down. I felt she did not want to come and that she had lied to me. I was very sad. I had been so excited about her coming that I was practically bouncing off the walls. But she never showed up.

My attitude toward the Hogsetts was now rebellious. I was not going to listen to anything they had to say about anything. I didn't care what they had to say about anything. In my mind, no matter what kept happening, I continued to believe my real mom would come soon and that was the day that I lived for.

My mom did come months later and she spent an afternoon with me at the Hogsetts home. I even went to her place once after that. I do not remember where that was, but it was a small apartment. I spent the day with her. At the end of the day she told me that I had to go home, back to the Hogsetts. I pleaded with her to let me stay, but she refused and insisted that I go back. She said that I had to go back but that she would visit me again.

When we got to the Hogsetts, I stood at their front gate, crying non-stop. Mom tried to encourage me to go to Jerry, who was kneeling down at the doorway with open arms and a smile, but I just stood there, frozen like a statue not wanting to move. Eventually my mom took me by the hand and literally dragged me over to Jerry. Once Jerry had a hold of me, my mom said she loved me and, tears welling up in her eyes, she left. I tried to break free and run after her, but Jerry held me close, telling me that everything would be fine. I ran into the house, went to my room and slammed the door. I had never felt so alone. I had never before felt such abandonment, such hopelessness, such betrayal.

There were many occasions like this with my mom. Most of the time she'd call and promise to come, but then she wouldn't. This happened so much that eventually Jerry and Suzanne, seeing my disappointment, stopped even telling me that she'd called or that she'd promised to come. That way I wouldn't get my hopes up, only to be let down in the end.

But the damage had been done. The feeling of abandonment over-whelmed me. My acting out at the Hogsetts would only get worse, no matter what they did to try to help me, no matter what they did to show me how much they loved me. I simply did not care. The woman who promised me that she'd come back for me had left me and disappeared again, perhaps for good this time. She swore over and over again that she loved me. But again she was gone. I found my mind sinking into a place I did not want it to be.

When my mom left through the front gate the last day she came to see me, she took with her all the trust I'd ever had. I could no longer believe anything she said. I could no longer rely on her words. Now, because my mom was gone and Suzanne was not my real mom and never could be, I wanted nothing, and I mean nothing, to do with the Hogsetts. I wanted my mom and she was the only person I cared about. I wanted her in spite of everything she had done. She was my mother.

Suzanne told me years later that my mom had called every Christmas in the wee hours of the morning. She was always so drunk Suzanne could hardly understand her. She asked to speak to me but was told "no" because it was the middle of the night and because she was drunk. When Suzanne would call her back the next day to ask if she wanted to talk to me then, she'd say she'd never called. Suzanne started recording her drunken calls and playing them back to her, telling her to call when she was sober, and that I'd like to hear from her. But she stopped calling after that.

One of my favorite pastimes was reading. As soon as I learned to read I'd sit in my room for hours or prop myself up against a tree in the backyard reading book after book. I sometimes even read the same book two or three times in just one day. Reading was my escape out of this world and into any make-believe world of my choosing. No matter how badly I thought things were going, I could leave it all behind and travel the seas, go exploring underground, or become part of a major battle in space. I loved it. I lived for it. I must have had more than 120 books to choose from in my personal library on my bookshelves at home. By age seven I was sometimes reading 200 to 300 page books in a day.

I also started to learn to play the trumpet in elementary school. I had a classical guitar my mom had brought me that I kept in my room as well. Playing music was another way for me to relieve stress and anger. I knew that some day I'd learn to play that guitar. I occasionally strummed it a few times, then set it back down. The guitar served as a reminder of my mom. I needed to protect it. I'd be damned if anyone else were to touch it or take it.

I had started having epileptic seizures shortly after coming to live with the Hogsetts at age five. Most of the seizures were called "petit mal," where I'd roll my eyes back for a brief second or two 20 or so times a day. During those few seconds I didn't know what was going on or that I was even having a seizure. Occasionally I'd have a "grand mal" seizure. My arms and legs would flail around uncontrollably and my whole body would shake violently. These would last a few minutes then just stop. After my first grand mal seizure my doctor prescribed Tegretol, a medication which helped prevent seizures, which worked quite well.

In 1987 I flew to Pennsylvania for Christmas to spend the holiday with Suzanne's mom and dad. Jerry and Suzanne were going to New Zealand for the holidays, and after several fruitless months of them pleading with me to go with them, they gave up. They then thought that I'd like to stay with Suzanne's parents for the holiday. But they were wrong. No matter what I'd told Jerry and Suzanne and no matter how I'd acted towards them, I really wanted to stay with them. I didn't want to spend another day with anyone I really didn't know. I don't know why, since I'd felt such anger and unhappiness living with the Hogsetts, I'd want to be with them and not with someone else.

Maybe it was because it was the holidays, because it was Christmas, that I wanted to be with someone familiar. Why couldn't these people get it? Why the heck was I getting shipped off again? And to top it off, I flew on the plane by myself! I was frightened flying alone and not knowing what the heck was going on. I had flown on planes before so I knew what it was like, but I had no idea where I was headed. They told me I'd be flying non-stop to Philadelphia, but I'd never heard of the place. It all felt so strange and creepy.

Jerry and Suzanne told me ahead of time that there was a flight attendant on the plane assigned to me to help me on and off the plane and to accompany me at all times. I had all the flight and arrival details and contact information attached to my shirt pocket with a big safety pin. But those details afforded me no comfort. I just knew I was being sent away to another strange place with more people I didn't know. I was being dumped again.

Jerry and Suzanne assured me over and over that I'd be coming back to them and that this was just a two-week vacation. But the little security I felt with them was no longer there. I didn't know who was going to protect me from strangers or from other danger when I was on the plane if they were not there. I was really angry at both of them and frightened, but the flight went smoothly. When we landed and I got off the plane in Philadelphia Suzanne's parents were there at the gate waiting for me. They both gave me a big hug and we drove off to their house. They seemed really happy to see me.

I stayed with them for two weeks. What I liked best was the fact that it snowed while I was there. I got to go sledding and play in the snow. I had a great time. There were some neighbors who had kids my age. When they heard I was there they came over and we started playing together. They invited me over to their house for hot cocoa and dinner. When we first met they asked where I was from. I told them I was a foster child from California and that I was here visiting my foster grandparents. When they asked what a foster child was, I told them it was someone sent to live in someone else's house because no one wanted them. That was what I thought at the time. I was still very confused about what was going to happen to me in the future. I was still hoping, against all odds, that my mom would come get me.

I actually enjoyed my time in Pennsylvania. In fact, when I boarded the plane to go back to California, I was crying. I seemed to have formed a small bond with Suzanne's father. He was a stamp collector and had shown me a little bit about how to collect stamps. He was always smiling and we even took walks together. Suzanne's mom however seemed very disinterested in me and always acted very distant. Strangely, I did not want to go back home. I did not know why, but I felt an emptiness inside, and for some reason I was afraid to go back to California. Maybe it was because the new friends I'd made in Pennsylvania did not know anything about my past and therefore did not judge me. Maybe it was because, even at age seven, I now felt more comfortable being with people I really did not know. I felt that if I didn't get close to people, I wouldn't risk losing them the way I'd lost my mother and sister. I think I cried myself to sleep on the plane. The next thing I knew we were landing in San Francisco.

Jerry and Suzanne were waiting for me as soon as I got off the plane. They both smothered me with big hugs and kisses and told me how much they'd missed me. Inside I felt empty. I lied to them and told them I'd missed them very much, but I really had not. In fact I hadn't missed them at all. But they believed me and to me that was good enough. That was the start of my lying to them in a big way. I started with little lies, and when they worked without a hitch, I told bigger lies. Lying became so easy for me that it became part of me. Lying allowed me to get whatever I wanted. Lying seemed to get me out of trouble. Lying seemed to be the solution to a great many things.

I was finally legally adopted by the Hogsetts in February 1988, just weeks before my eighth birthday. The Hogsetts asked me a few weeks before going to the courthouse to sign the adoption papers if I liked being with them and if I wanted them to adopt me. I told them that I didn't. When they asked me why, I said it was because there were too many chores and too much homework for me to do at their house. Suzanne explained to me that no matter where I went that there would be chores and responsibilities. That was all part of growing up.

After she said that I told her I was willing to be adopted. However, in reality, I did not want to be adopted by them. I did not want to be adopted by anyone. I wanted to go back to my mom. I was waiting for her to come back to get me like she promised. I figured that if I were adopted, then my mom would never be able to get me back. I was angry and frustrated because I felt no one would listen to me. Why would no one listen to me? Why was I being made to do something I did not want to do? Why couldn't the Hogsetts see that my mom would be coming back for me and that adopting me was not the answer?

I wanted to be able to do what I wanted when I wanted to. I did not want this structure of chores, homework, rules, being told to calm down, or being told to go to my room. I wanted power and control over my own life. When I did not have that control I felt completely backed into a corner and powerless over what might happen.

I missed my sister too. I was very lonely at the Hogsetts' house. But I said, "Yes, I want to be adopted." I said yes because I could see in Suzanne's eyes that adopting me was something she really wanted, something she was so excited about. I did not want to hurt Jerry and Suzanne by telling them what I really wanted, so I told them yes. They were very happy.

A few weeks later we went to the courthouse and I sat in a courtroom with a judge, my social worker Hale, and the Hogsetts. The judge asked me how I was doing and if I'd like to be adopted by the Hogsetts. I told him that I was doing well and that I enjoyed living with them. After filling out a few more papers, the judge said it was official. I was adopted. Then we all went to a restaurant to celebrate.

My legal name was now Jessie Romine Hogsett. I was officially starting my new life with a new family. I knew what adoption meant. It meant my mom Leanne was not coming for me. I knew now with certainty that I was not going to be picked up by my mom and be taken away to live in the world I'd dreamed up and fantasized about for so many years. I knew that I now had new parents, that Jerry and Suzanne were my new mom and dad.

Since the adoption was final, I knew that even if my mom did come, I now had a new family and she could do nothing about it. I thought, "OK, another chapter in my life." A new beginning. I guessed I'd see what would happen and where it would go. I still did not understand why I had to be adopted. I did not understand why my mom had not come. I did not understand why I couldn't be with my sister. I did not understand a lot of things that were happening. I was upset, sad, confused, hurt and unsure how I'd now cope. I felt I had no voice in a world of confusion, in a world where no one heard me, in a world where my cries for help fell on deaf ears.

The Hogsetts knew when they adopted me that I came with many serious medical problems as well as behavioral issues resulting from the abuse and neglect I'd endured. They still agreed to adopt me anyway and were ready to try to give me a life that otherwise I would never have had. That really said a lot about who they were.

At the time elementary school was hard for me. I did not feel that I fit in. I remember seeing my schoolmates on the playground, laughing, running, and having fun. For some reason I stayed in the background. I was still soiling my underpants, even at age eight. The kids smelled the odor emanating from me, then made comments and teased me about it. It made me so angry and hurt at the same time. I also had a wide ten-inch scar running vertically on the top of my head from four early childhood hydrocephalus surgeries. Hair didn't grow on top of the scar so it was impossible to hide it. This too was a target for kids to tease me. They always said I had a fish hook, or that I had some disease.

Then there was my last name, Hogsett. "Oh look, there goes the hog," they'd say. The teasing went on non-stop. I remember often coming home with my head down and quietly coming through the door. Jerry said that all kids tease and that this unfortunately would go on until they grew up. I of course did not believe him. I thought that I was the problem. I also thought I'd be teased mercilessly like this for the rest of my life so the rest of my life would be miserable too. I buried myself even deeper in reading the books in my room in order to escape the harsh reality around me.

I did have a good friend however in elementary school. His name was Justin. I never had more than one good friend at a time. I never seemed to get along with the other kids. I really didn't feel at ease being around the other boys at school. I was fascinated by the girls however. I even chased some of the pretty girls around school, catching up to them and kissing them on their cheeks. They freaked out for some reason and ran and told the teachers. This got me in trouble. Then Dad and Suzanne would get a phone call from the school. But I craved the attention, good or bad. Most of the time however, the attention I got was negative attention.

When I reached the third grade I started playing the trumpet in school. My dad rented a trumpet for me so I could give it a try. My mouth was really small and I had an overbite the size of a horse. I had braces on my teeth to boot. Although it was far from easy, I started to play the trumpet or I at least attempted to in my garage at home.

When the first day of lessons with the other kids came, the music teacher told us to play a simple scale. Everyone started to play and it sounded somewhat like we were doing something right. However, I was confused. I had the trumpet lesson book open. I saw what was in front of me, but I could not understand where it showed how to play the notes. I remember asking the teacher. He said to just follow the black dots on the page underneath the notes and that he'd show me which keys to hold down in order to play each note. I was still confused. Everyone was playing but me. I started to have tears in my eyes. By the end of the lesson I was ready to give up. I left in a hurry and walked home.

The next week the music class had practice again. I had not picked up my trumpet to practice since the first day of lessons. I hadn't even looked at it. I came back to the music class because Jerry told me not to give up and to keep asking the music teacher for help if I needed it. I opened the lesson book to the page the teacher told us to find. He told us to start playing a simple C scale. I lifted my trumpet up, lifted the mouthpiece to my mouth, and began to press the keys. At first it sounded like just noise. But I kept trying to read what the instruction book said and to look at my fingers on the keys at the same time. Pretty soon the other kids stopped playing but I continued. When I finished, the teacher and all my classmates started to clap. For some reason, all of a sudden, I got it. Just like that, I got it. I could play.

I played so well the teacher told me that if it weren't so late in the school year, he'd recommend me as a trumpet player in the local High School band. I couldn't believe it. I couldn't believe that just weeks before I couldn't play a single note. And now I was such a natural the teacher said I was good enough to play with the big boys! It felt so good to hear that. I had never heard such exuberant praise before in my life, praise for a talent I had. For someone to think so highly of something I did at age eight was amazing. I was so happy! But I said nothing in return, not a thing. I didn't know what to say. I didn't know how to react. In fact I felt really uncomfortable, out of place. So instead, I smiled and just left when the class was over. I then started practicing every day in my garage at home.

My dad then bought the trumpet for me. Yes, I said, "My dad." By this time I was able to start to form a relationship with Jerry. As I'd never had a father figure in my life, it seemed easy for me to warm up to him. As for Suzanne, I felt I already had a mother and that was Leanne. She was Mom and no other woman could ever take her place. I could not bring myself to be close to any other woman who tried to step in and take over her role. I was not going to allow that. That was something that I had complete control over.

I was happy the trumpet was mine. I continued to play it throughout elementary school and into middle school. I played in the marching band, the jazz band, the symphonic band and the Palo Alto All City Honor Band. I became the top trumpet player in each of these groups. Even in elementary school I understood that playing an instrument and loving music were new ways for me to escape reality and to express my feelings.

When I reached the third grade, I struggled to understand some subjects in school. Lonnie, my third grade teacher, was a friend of

Suzanne's and a really nice man. He always asked me how I was doing and he always seemed to care what I had to say and how I was feeling. We talked about school things and about my life outside of school. I felt I could let my guard down a little with him because he knew nothing about my past and he was easy to talk to. He had a non-threatening manner and was soft-spoken, gentle and easy going. It also seemed easier for me to talk to a man than a woman.

Our class participated in what the school called a Read-O-Rama, where we read books on our own and then told the teacher about them. The more pages the book had the better. We got a sticker for each book we read. Each sticker was a different color, which represented the number of pages in the book.

I loved to read. I told my teacher Lonnie that I read a 300 page book a day, every day. The fact was that I didn't. I picked books from the classroom bookshelf and took them to Lonnie. I told him that I'd just finished the book. By reading the back of the book before I took it to him, I was able to put together a summary and add a few other little ideas from what I read on the back that sounded right. Lonnie fell for my trick hook, line and sinker. I got more stickers than anyone else. In fact Dad and Suzanne even promised me fifty dollars if I read the most books in my class.

My trick worked for a while. I was getting so much praise from my teacher, from Dad and Suzanne, and from other kids at school. I felt like I was the most popular kid in class. I held my head high. It seemed like nothing bad could happen.

My game was short lived however, because my luck ran out. One of the books I took up to Lonnie was a book he'd just read the week before. So when I summarized for him what I thought sounded good, he knew right then and there I'd just made it up. When he confronted me about it I got very defensive and continued to lie. I told him I had no idea what he was talking about. I pleaded and pleaded with him to believe me and I swore I'd read the book. I even told him that if he didn't believe me, then maybe he didn't read the book. No matter what I said or tried, it didn't work. Getting caught in this lie ultimately led to more anger and frustration. My schoolwork, social life and problems with my parents got worse after that.

I began to lie even more because I wanted to feel that praise. I wanted people to think I was someone without problems. Sure, lying started as a game to me in order to get positive reactions and to control situations. But after a while it just became second nature. It seemed that if I lied I could get whatever I wanted. In my mind it seemed that I never did anything right. By lying I thought other people would think I was a good kid. They'd think I could succeed at anything they asked me to do. This would work as long as they never found out the truth. But I was so wrong.

Between the ages of eight and ten home life was rough to say the least. I started to develop coping skills to try to deal with my anger and the feeling of helplessness. I started to learn how to really manipulate people in order to get anything I wanted. I played one person against another. I threw my lunch away all the time on the way to school, then told the teachers I had no food because my parents didn't make my lunch. Then I'd get school food, which I liked better than the lunch my parents had made for me. All I had to do was say what people wanted to hear or tell lies to complete strangers in order to get what I wanted.

My lying became more blatant and my defiance became even more brazen. I was also very sneaky with almost everything. I'd watch TV when I wasn't supposed to. I'd shove everything under my bed and tell my parents my room was clean. I'd hide things that I knew I wasn't supposed to have. I'd go into my parents' room and look through their things just because I thought I was entitled to. I did not care.

I also started stealing big time. If I didn't get something I wanted right away, I'd find a way to steal it. I didn't just steal from Dad and Suzanne. I stole from kids at school when they were playing in the schoolyard. I'd go to the school office to see what was in the lost and found that I wanted. I'd say it was mine and they'd give it to me. None of my friends were off limits either. I'd even steal from them. Nothing was safe from my grasp. It didn't occur to me at all that my actions were hurting anyone else. I was so emotionless by then that I could not relate to how anything I did had any effect whatsoever on anybody.

One morning, as I walked to school, the sun was out and there was a light breeze. I walked alone as I did every morning. School was nearby, only a few blocks away. I saw a car parked along the sidewalk about a block from school. As I looked closely at it, I noticed the doors were unlocked. I looked to see if anyone was around and, seeing no one, I proceeded to open the car door. I sat down in the passenger seat and opened the glove box. Inside was a mint tin full of change. I took it, closed the car door, and began to walk the rest of the way to school.

Suddenly, behind me, I heard a yell. A man ran out of a house across the street, caught up to me, and grabbed my arm. He seemed very agitated. He wanted to know why I was in his car and what I had taken. I denied everything even though he said he had watched me from the upstairs window of his house. I told him I didn't take anything, but he didn't believe me. He walked me the rest of the way to school and right up to the school office. I held my head down as we entered. I sat in a chair in the office while he was talking to the woman standing behind a counter. Then the principal came out and asked me to join him and the man in his office.

The principal was a nice man I thought. He never raised his voice. He always had a way of making the kids feel at home when talking to him, no matter what the situation was. He asked me why I was in the car. I just shrugged my shoulders and didn't answer. I kept my head down because I didn't want to look him in the eye. He asked me if I had taken anything and he told me to empty my pockets. I pulled out the mint tin and silently placed it on his desk. The man confirmed the mint tin was his, said something briefly to the principal, and left. After he left the principal explained that what I'd done was not acceptable and that he'd be calling my parents at home. Then he sent me to my third grade class.

As I was walking to class I knew that I didn't want the school day to end. I dreaded going home to face Dad and Suzanne. I was really scared!

I even thought for a while that after school I'd just run away from home and that would settle everything. I walked into class and sat down. Lonnie knew that there was something bothering me. He asked me throughout the day if I were OK. I'd just nod yes and half smile. I was just going through the motions, pretending. I had already turned the art of making a false smile into a science.

When the school day ended I left school and on the way home I thought again about running away. But for some reason I could not. I walked home very slowly, worrying about what was going to happen when I got there. I wondered what Dad and Suzanne would say and what they would do. I was afraid I was going to be lectured. I was afraid I was going to be sent to my room. I was afraid I was going to be hit, even though they had never hit me. I was used to being hit a lot when I was younger, so the fear was ingrained. I was never embarrassed about being caught stealing, just sometimes afraid of what the punishment might be. Then I thought, who cares.

I knew what I had done was wrong because I knew stealing was wrong, but I still felt compelled to do it. It was as if some force told me to get into that car and violate someone's space. I did not think about the consequences. My impulse control was non-existent. I was unable to understand that what I was doing hurt other people. I did not care if I hurt other people. I wanted to have things my own way. After all, why should I care about anyone else when it seemed that no one cared about me? I had learned before I came to live with the Hogsetts how to take care of myself. I did not need anyone telling me what to do or how to live.

When I reached my house I was immediately confronted by Suzanne. My dad was at work but I was assured that he already knew about the incident and would be talking to me when he got home. Suzanne asked me why I got into the car. I felt confused because I just didn't know. Things just happened and I didn't know why I did them.

Of course that was not the answer she was looking for. She told me that I must know and she asked me again. I told her again that I didn't know. I began to get angry and defensive. I threw my hands out to my sides in a gesture as if to say, "What else do you want me to say?" Deep inside I knew that in that car there had to be something I wanted, and there was. There was money. But I wasn't going to tell her that. I couldn't tell her that. It was almost as if my lips were frozen, preventing me from telling her what I was thinking.

I was sent to my room and told to stay there until my father came home. Wow, father! That was emphasized and I immediately felt scared. I went to my room and sat in the corner far away from the door as if trying to hide from anyone coming into the room. The fact was, if I had a lot of money, I had control. I had independence. I had freedom. I could buy friends with money, and if I could buy friends, I wouldn't feel so alone.

My dad came home from work and talked to me in my room. He had a very stern look on his face and he seemed really mad. He raised his voice at times to make sure he got his point across. I held my head down most of the time, as I really could not look at him. I could not face him. I was too scared to do that. I did not want him to see me starting to cry. To me that was a sign of weakness and I could not let anyone see that. I had built an imaginary wall around me in order to hide my true feelings from everyone out there. And I was determined not to let anyone break that down.

I was just happy the day was over. My defiance and my "I don't care" attitude at school would continue throughout elementary school. I made it clear to Dad and Suzanne that I no longer wanted to go to that school and that I wanted to go to another school. Then my third grade teacher Lonnie talked to me about it. He was calm and on my level, getting down on his knees so he was around my height. This eased the tension level. He also empathized with what I was going through. He assured me that I had what it took to succeed in this school. I felt that he was really concerned about me and I liked that. I really had an easy time talking to him. For some reason it was easier for me to talk to people like Lonnie who I really didn't have a close relationship with, than with people I did have one with.

Dad and Suzanne did lots of activities with me. I especially liked the things Dad and I did together. These were what I thought of as boy things — things like building Matchbox cars, making Science Fair projects, and playing Frisbee. But since he knew me so well and knew what I was like, I felt ill at ease confiding in him. I was afraid of getting attached to people. I knew that people not close to me would not judge me, and I didn't have to see them on a regular basis. And if I weren't attached to them, I did not have to fear losing them. I also knew that because people I was not close to did not know about my misbehaving, it was easier for me to fool them. It was easier to trick them into believing I was the good, honest, well-mannered, sweet child they wanted me to be.

That of course was a complete cover-up for the person I really was. Lonnie wanted to know why I wanted to change schools. I told him it was because I felt I did not fit in at this school. I was unhappy there. He assured me that, if I went to another school, in time I might have the same feelings I had now. He encouraged me to stay put. He said I'd be missed if I chose to go to another school. In the end I agreed to stay. He always let me know he was available anytime I needed someone to talk to. I finished the third, fourth and fifth grades at Palo Verde School. Middle school started with grade six.

Making friends was also a struggle for me. I really did not know how to be part of a group of kids. All the teasing I had endured in school made me not want to hang out with other kids. My trust and attachment issues prevented me from forming relationships with kids my age. I seemed to struggle with trying to find an identity. I'd see a group of kids I wanted to hang out with, but when I tried to talk to them, I had no idea how to act or what to say. Most of the time I was mean to them. I thought that was how I was supposed to act. After all, acting tough seemed a sure-fire way for me to be safe from any threats. It also prevented me from getting close to anyone.

Another problem with making friends was that in order to be accepted by the kids who did want to be around me, it seemed I'd have to become their scapegoat. I'd have to do things for them that they knew were wrong. They'd tell me to do them because I'd then be the one to get in trouble and not them. These were things like stealing from other kids, teasing them, and keeping items like electronic games for them which they weren't supposed to have at school. I did this because that's what they asked me to do. I thought if I did these things that I'd then be accepted. But I was sadly mistaken. Every time I was caught I was the one who got in trouble. The other kids denied everything and got off scot free. This of course fueled my anger and frustration even more.

I did manage, however, to make friends with kids who seemed to exhibit the same defiant behaviors I did. They were in the same grade I was and were about my age. I could relate to them, to how they felt, and to the things they did. These friendships were in my comfort zone.

Dad and Suzanne often took me to the park and encouraged me to play with the other kids on the playground. But I preferred to sit alone in the sand box, wade alone in the shallow pool, swing alone on the swings, or just sit alone on the bench near my parents. Dad and Suzanne often got frustrated and asked me why I wasn't playing with the other kids. I just told them that I wanted to be alone or that I didn't feel like asking the other kids if I could play with them. I felt anguish deep inside. I wanted more than anything to have cool friends and be part of the groups of kids enjoying themselves. But I just couldn't bring myself to make the first attempt. When my parents starting asking other kids if they wanted to play with me, I told them not to. I was just too embarrassed. I didn't want to reach out, to venture out, to risk rejection by kids who weren't like me.

Sure I was shy, but it was more than that. I wanted to have fun but I just couldn't bring myself to engage in activities like playing tag, basketball or anything else that involved playing with a group of kids. I joined the Cub Scouts, which I enjoyed somewhat. I earned a number of achievement badges for successfully completing various projects. I reveled in the praise I got from that. Earning the badges gave me a sense of accomplishment and personal gratification. Dad would often give me a hand with the projects so I could earn the badges. I appreciated his help, which consisted mostly of guidance. I did the actual work myself in order to earn the badges. The other kids in my Cub Scout den seemed to enjoy being around me. They did not know anything about my past and never asked me to do things I was not supposed to do. I felt accepted and that felt good.

Something that really bugged me was both Dad and Suzanne always trying to take photos of all of us together as a family. Since I rarely felt they were my family, why should I pretend? I was hesitant and often never smiled. I really didn't like my picture taken and never saw any good reason for it. Suzanne always pleaded with me to smile, but I wouldn't. I figured if I didn't smile I wouldn't have to have my picture taken. Then I wouldn't have to put on a fake smile. I wouldn't have to pretend I was a happy child. They succeeded in getting a lot of pictures of me by myself, most often complete with fake smile. But I think they rarely succeeded in getting a photo of all three of us together.

Suzanne was in the travel business. She was a tour leader and took groups all over the U.S. and to many different countries. She was also in the process of starting her own travel consulting business that she ran out of our house. She told me she was doing this so she could be home more with me. I remember her bringing home all kinds of things she'd collected on her many trips. They were souvenirs like earrings, pottery, fabrics, clothes, paintings, special coins, foreign money, masks, post cards, books, and music. She always took lots of photos to show us too.

Once she even came to my elementary school and was a guest speaker in my class. She told us about her trip to Australia. She brought a humongous map of Australia to show. She also brought a stuffed animal, an Australian koala. She taught our class some fun Australian words. The class giggled and laughed and she was a big hit with them. I was surprised to see her there and it was a cool feeling.

Because of her travel business our summer vacations were not your average summer vacations. We did not go to Disneyland, Magic

Mountain, Sea World, go visit relatives, or do anything that it seemed normal families did in the summer.

Sure, we went camping and we went to places like SeaWorld and Disneyland, but usually not in the middle of summer. Instead, on our summer vacations we went to Europe and beyond! We headed out for long periods to points unknown, or at least unknown to me. In Europe I climbed the Leaning Tower of Pisa, island hopped in Greece by ferry, and took cable cars to the tops of mountains in Switzerland. At age 12 I went to the Auschwitz concentration camp in Poland, which was eerie and really creeped me out. I still remember to this day so many great things we did on our travels.

On one of our first trips together we flew to Belgrade, Yugoslavia. After being awake all night with jet lag and a midnight to dawn construction crew jack-hammering up the pavement next to our hotel, I was dragged to see the castle. It felt like I'd walked for miles over uneven cobblestone walkways. In reality I hadn't walked that far, but it sure seemed like it. When I looked down at the castle's moat I thought I'd much rather be swimming in it, or better yet, fishing in it, than climbing seemingly forever up the cobblestone steps. In Europe I liked England and Austria the best because they had a lot of countryside and so reminded me the most of home.

In Turkey I liked going in the mosques and helping Suzanne shop for things in the bazaars. Everything always smelled so good there and people stopped and talked to me because I was such a rarity. Few parents traveled there with their children. They always told me how lucky I was to be able to come to their country. But I didn't feel lucky. I didn't appreciate anything we were seeing or doing.

I liked to laugh, although times where I let loose and laughed a lot were few and far between. I do remember a few funny things that happened. What I remember most about our visit to Turkey was staying in a cave hotel in Cappadocia, in central Turkey. The caves were two-thousand years old. Some were fitted out as small hotels, with basic but comfortable rooms. Our cave room came with large fake tiger patterned bedspreads draped loosely over the beds. Dad grabbed one of these, wrapped himself up in it, and walked out in front of the cave so Suzanne could take his picture. He looked just like a cave man. I thought it was the silliest thing I'd ever seen.

We went on an African safari, where one night I saw two male lions just sitting in the road in front of our Land Rover. We waited there in the dark, with our headlights shining clearly on them until, about ten minutes later, they sauntered off into the bush. I made friends with our driver and with the Africans who worked at the safari camp. I loved the outdoors, the open spaces, the freedom from any daily routine, and the fun of looking for wild animals hiding in the bush. In Sydney, Australia, I thought the Opera House in Sydney Harbor was really neat. But even better was taking the ferry across the harbor to the Sydney Zoo, where we saw koalas and kangaroos.

In India I was frightened by the large crowds. They made me nervous because I was afraid someone would grab me. The heat made me tired and lethargic. In Calcutta of all places, I was so tired of traveling that I fell asleep during a rickshaw ride through town. I don't know how I did that, but I did.

But my favorite experience by far was the trip Suzanne and I took together to Costa Rica. It was just the two of us. We took boat rides in the jungle, saw crocodiles, chased huge brilliant butterflies in the rainforest, went to the beach, swam in the hotel pool, rode horses, and saw a real erupting volcano. The best part of the trip was the undivided attention I got from Suzanne. She did nothing but pay constant attention to me. She did nothing but what I wanted to do, all day, every day.

I also cherished the trips where I shared common interests with my dad, like an astronomy trip to Glacier Point in Yosemite National Park. We stayed up late into the night and saw the pitch black sky peppered with more stars than I'd ever seen. About 40 people were there with all sorts of telescopes and binoculars. It was great! My dad also took me to the Gilroy Garlic Festival, where we camped overnight. These were very special outings for me, ones which helped me feel closer to him, to attach to him.

These were all memorable trips. But most of the time I wanted instead to just stay home in the safety of my bedroom. I wanted to stay where I was familiar with everything around me. I wouldn't be shy about letting Dad and Suzanne know before heading out on pretty much any long trip, that I just didn't want to go.

Sometimes when I didn't want to go on the long overseas trips I wouldn't go. At other times I didn't want to go, but as the trip neared Dad and Suzanne convinced me to change my mind. It made me feel pushed around. I agreed to go to make them happy and to stop them constantly asking me why I didn't want to go. But for the trips I downright refused to go on, they'd hire a child sitter to watch me and take care of me while they were away.

The sitters were sometimes people whose references were checked out and who were interviewed by Dad and Suzanne. At other times they were people my dad knew from work. I always looked forward to having the sitters come. To me this was a time when I could do pretty much as I pleased and get away with a lot more than I could when Dad and Suzanne were home. Since I did not have a relationship with the sitters, I was cautious around them. Of course the risk of being caught doing something really bad and then having Dad and Suzanne find out about it still did not deter me from doing exactly as I pleased. It didn't stop me from manipulating anyone I needed to in order to get my way. When Dad and Suzanne left to go on their trips the sitter was always there before they left. She'd stay at the house with me full time, day and night. Some of them would go to work when I went to school.

I played Little League baseball at the time. At age nine I was in the "pitching machine" age group. A machine pitched the balls to the batter instead of a real pitcher throwing them from the mound. Because of my hydrocephalus the doctor advised me to wear a batting helmet at all times when playing, even when I was playing in the outfield. This was to prevent me from getting hurt if a baseball hit me in the head. I hated wearing that helmet because it made me feel so different from the other kids. I felt like an outsider, even a laughing stock.

As a result, I was the focus of much teasing from some of the other kids, both those on my team and on the teams we played. I think even a few parents snickered here and there. They didn't understand why I had to wear the helmet. My teammates knew why and most supported me by cheering me on and telling me that, with or without the helmet, they appreciated my being on their team. However, even though my team-mates knew about my condition, a few still poked fun at me every now and then.

Once when a sitter stayed with me, she had no idea I had to wear a helmet. I felt no need to tell her. It was something Dad and Suzanne had forgotten to mention to her and I was sure going to capitalize on that. Well, as you might have guessed, during the next game I got hit in the head with a baseball that was batted straight in my direction. It really hurt. My vision started to get blurry and I instantly got a massive headache. The coach came over and asked if I were OK. I told him I was. I sat out the rest of the game on the bench. Then the sitter took me to the hospital to have me checked out. My head turned out to be OK. But even after that incident I was still dead set against wearing the helmet any time I didn't have to. I just could not bear to be belittled and made fun of.

Another time when a sitter stayed with me, I pretended I was going to school. I got out of bed, got dressed and ate breakfast. I placed my backpack by the front door with my books and homework in it. My lunch was packed and in the refrigerator from the night before. I put the lunch in my backpack, then threw the right strap over my shoulder and headed out. The sitter told me to have a great day in school. I then pretended to walk to school. Shortly afterwards she left to go to work.

After I figured she'd left, instead of walking the rest of the way to school, I turned around and walked back home. Even though the house was locked, I knew where the spare key was hidden and I was able to get right back in. I had seen my dad hide the key one day and never let on I knew where it was. Once inside I realized that as soon as the school found out I wasn't there, the house phone would ring. That was the standard thing for the school to do. They didn't wait until the end of the day to notify parents that their child hadn't come to school. The school called the parents as soon as they found out a child was absent.

I decided I'd try to disguise my voice in order to sound like an adult. I'd say Jessie was sick and apologize for not calling them. The plan was all set. If I could pull this off, then there was no way Dad and Suzanne would ever know and I could pretty much do what I wanted all day without fear of reprimand.

The phone rang and, as I expected, it was the school. I answered in the deepest voice I could muster up at age nine. It worked because they called me Mr. Hogsett and told me that they hoped my son would feel better soon. I hung up the phone. It worked! I couldn't believe it. It was so easy. I sat in Dad and Suzanne's big bed, smiling, then pondering what I was going to do first. I didn't yet know that what would happen later that day would ultimately foil my plan for the perfect day.

I started off my new adventure by going through the kitchen cupboards, looking to see what kinds of sweet treats were possibly in there for me to eat. I found some sugary fruit snacks and a box of Kudos granola bars coated in chocolate. They were so good. I ate five of them in an hour, then turned on the TV and found a station showing cartoons. I was only allowed to watch TV an hour or so a day, and then only after all my homework was done. And most of the shows I was allowed to watch had to be educational. Now I had my freedom. I loved it. I sat on the couch and propped my feet up on the coffee table. I did not have a care in the world at that point.

After about an hour of watching cartoons I decided to go see what Dad and Suzanne had hidden in their room. I was fascinated mainly with things I did not have or was not allowed to have. Anything that looked cool to me I wanted. Also money. I knew that if I had money I could buy whatever I wanted. My allowance didn't buy all that much. As I looked through Dad and Suzanne's stuff I found a few dollars in Suzanne's nightstand drawers next to her side of their bed. I took that, then found a pocket knife in my dad's nightstand. I thought, "Wow, that looks like fun." I wanted it, so I just took it and put it in my pocket. I also pocketed a few pieces of candy that my dad always seemed to have in containers on top of his nightstand. Then I went to the garage where my bike was, hopped on, and rode the mile or so to the variety store downtown.

When I arrived I left my bike outside the store, hiding it behind some bushes. I had a bike lock but did not have anything to attach it to. I figured the bike would be safe since it was sitting in front of the store and it was hidden. After all, it was daytime and I'd only be in the store for a short time. I walked in and went right to the toy section. I found a cap gun, which I paid for with the money I had stolen from Suzanne. I wanted the cap gun because Dad and Suzanne didn't like guns, even toy guns. I wanted something that I was not allowed to have. The lady behind the counter asked me why I wasn't in school. I told her that my dad said I could stay home for the day because I was just getting over being sick. She smiled and told me that she hoped I'd feel better. I said thanks and left.

When I walked outside, my bike was gone. I thought maybe I was looking in the wrong spot, but there was only one short row of bushes in front of the store. My bike clearly was not there. I began to panic, not so much because my bike was probably gone, but because now I'd have to explain to Dad and Suzanne how I lost it.

I went back inside the store and told the clerk who'd helped me earlier with my purchase. She told me to call the police and make a report that my bike was probably stolen. I called and made a phone report, giving the policeman a description of the bike. He didn't ask why I wasn't in school. He said they'd come look for it and if they found it they'd bring it to my house. I just hoped they'd find it before Dad and Suzanne got home.

I started to cry because all of a sudden I was really frightened. Then I wondered how I was going to get home. I knew I had only one option. I called my dad's friend Len to see if he could pick me up. I picked up the store phone and dialed his number. Fortunately Dad and Suzanne had given me emergency numbers to call in case I needed help. When Len answered I told him that I'd ridden my bike to the store and that it had been stolen. When he came to pick me up I pleaded with him to take me home and not to tell Dad and Suzanne what had happened. He said that they needed to know so he had no choice. But he agreed to wait until they got home from their trip to talk to them. That wouldn't be for at least another two weeks. OK, I thought, that will give me enough time to make up a good story to tell them as to why I did what I did. Len took me home and stayed with me until my sitter arrived.

Later that day a policeman showed up at my home, and, luckily for me, he had my bike. He said he'd found it behind the store hidden behind a dumpster. I was so relieved. I thanked him and he left. At least my bike was back. That would be one less thing I'd have to explain to Dad and Suzanne. In my mind, after getting my bike back, I felt that everything that had happened that day would turn out all right. I knew I'd be in trouble for skipping school. But now Dad and Suzanne wouldn't learn about the stolen money or the cap gun I'd bought with it, and I sure wasn't going to tell them. I just put all this in the back of my mind and decided that I'd deal with it when they returned.

As I grew older, days like this became more and more common. My stealing got worse and my lying so frequent that Dad and Suzanne could not trust anything I said. I enjoyed stealing. I enjoyed the fact that the money was so easy for me to get and that I could buy what I wanted. No one else existed in my mind and I really did not care who was hurt in the process, as long as I was happy.

Even when I did tell the truth, few people believed me. I even told Dad and Suzanne on several occasions that if they didn't believe me I'd take a lie detector test to prove what I was saying. They always said that wouldn't be possible because they thought I literally believed everything I said. And since I believed my lies, they were convinced I could then pass a lie detector test.

There were many times Suzanne left her purse on the dining room table or on a chair, table or sofa in the living room. When she went down the hall to the toilet or she got in the shower, I'd open her wallet and take twenty dollars here, five dollars there. It did not matter. I felt an urge to steal money and I honestly did not know why. Even if my real mother had come back to get me and taken me home to live with her as she'd promised, I'd have stolen from her as well. Part of me wanted to stop, but another part of me thought stealing was fun and easy. It was almost as if a voice inside my head was telling me to do these things and I was powerless to do anything about it.

Soon I wasn't worried about getting caught or even if I were hurting anyone. It no longer crossed my mind. I just wanted what I wanted and I wanted it now! Even the neighbor kids I played with were not safe from my ways. I stole money from them too. One day Suzanne found out I was stealing. She spotted a new toy in my backpack and wondered where it had come from. I told her that I had stolen money from my friend down the street while I was at his house playing one day. Then I'd bought the toy with the money. I did not feel any shame. Instead, I was really upset because I was forced to apologize to my friend face to face. I was furious that Dad and Suzanne made me return the money too. How dare they?

My lying and stealing were getting worse and by middle school both had gotten out of hand. I started sixth grade at Jane Lathrop Stanford Middle School in Palo Alto. This was a completely different kind of school than I was used to. It must have been at least five times the size of my elementary school. There were classrooms and halls leading everywhere. The place was huge. There were kids everywhere! The new school was very intimidating, because now I saw lots of older and bigger kids that I'd have to deal with.

Here I felt vulnerable. I was extremely shy. Although I was very tall for my age, I was rail thin and didn't work out, so I didn't have much muscle tone. As such, the other boys didn't see me as any type of force to reckon with. This was also the first time I'd go to different classes with different teachers throughout the day. It was unlike elementary school, where I'd stayed in the same classroom all day with the same teacher.

Fortunately my few friends from elementary school ended up in my new classes and they helped me cope.

I still played the trumpet in middle school and did very well at it. Playing it continued to be a good outlet for my anger, sadness, and loneliness. I also started taking a keen interest in girls, so I started caring a lot about how I looked. The problem was that I couldn't muster up the courage to approach any girls. I just watched them from a distance, wondering what it would be like to have a girlfriend.

I started showing the first signs of going through puberty at age nine and a half, so now my feelings for girls were really intensified. I knew where my dad kept his stash of Playboy magazines in the garage. I often went out there and picked out one or two. I took them to my room, looked at them and imagined what it would be like to be with a girl and see her naked. Wowee! I even tried to sell some of Dad's Playboys to the other kids at school in order to earn a few extra dollars and to hopefully make some new friends in the process.

One night I got back-to-back phone calls from a number of kids wanting to know if I were still selling the Playboys and wondering how much they cost. Dad and Suzanne were in the same room as the phone and could hear me talk, so I really couldn't give out any information. I acted like I was just talking to a friend wanting to know about homework. The next day the boys asked why I acted the way I had and I told them. They laughed, but soon they stopped calling. I never sold any Playboys, no matter how hard I tried.

6 Buying friends

I kept striving to make friends and wanting to be popular in school. Dad and Suzanne had fixed up a room in their house, turning it into their computer room and office. New cabinets lined the walls, including one that locked. They always hid the key to the locking cabinet and I never knew where it was until one day I saw Dad put it in a drawer. When they went out for dinner one night and left me alone in the house (they felt I was old enough to be left alone for a few hours then, at age 10), I went into their office, got the key and tried it in the cabinet locks. Bingo! It opened the big cabinet. Inside there were piles of travel business papers. But there was also something else, something that caught my eye. It was a cigar box. Before I opened it I thought to myself, "Hey, I might just try to smoke one of those."

I had tried smoking a cigarette several months earlier while tagging along with Dad and Suzanne to a travel class Suzanne was teaching at a San Francisco university. The first time I tried smoking, I felt a strange tingling sensation throughout my body. I became completely relaxed at that very moment. I felt like a totally different person, an independent person, and that felt good. So I thought that smoking a cigar might give me that same feeling.

When I opened the box there were no cigars. Instead I could not believe what I saw. I had struck the jackpot! Inside was a stack of 20, 50 and 100 dollar bills. My eyes grew huge. My heart started to pound. So many thoughts went through my mind. I just stood there staring at it all. Then it occurred to me that there was so much money in there that Dad and Suzanne would never miss it if I just took a 20. So just like that I pocketed a 20 dollar bill, closed and locked the cabinet, and put the key back. I left the room, went into the living room and turned on the TV.

When Dad and Suzanne were due to come home, I put a cold rag on top of the TV to cool it down. I was not supposed to watch TV when they were gone. They did not want me watching violent programs, as I was prone to have nightmares after seeing violence on TV. I was also supposed to be doing my homework. So I thought that by putting a cold rag on top of the TV, that I'd be able to keep them from feeling the heat it generated. I brushed my teeth, then crawled into bed. I heard Dad and Suzanne come in and then heard Suzanne tell Dad that it didn't seem like I'd watched TV. My trick worked. I was really proud of myself.

I was still awake but I closed my eyes as I heard them coming down the hall to check on me. I liked playing possum. I kept asking myself what I was going to spend that 20 dollars on. I was so excited. The next day I got up as usual and got ready for school. Because they'd come home late Dad and Suzanne were still asleep when I left the house and started to walk to school. On the way there I stopped at a grocery store and bought some candy with the 20 dollars. At school I passed the candy out to some girls I wanted to get to know. I thought, "Hey, if I give them something then maybe they'll notice me and start to like me." It seemed to work. I got "Hellos" and smiles from the girls who walked by. I was feeling quite special. But I wanted more. I really wanted to make an impression.

I continued stealing money from the cigar box for many months to come — 20 dollars here and 20 dollars there. Then one day I took a 100 dollar bill. I took it from the middle of the wad of cash in the cigar box. I thought Dad and Suzanne wouldn't be able to tell if I did that. When I got to school the next day I literally started handing out money to the girls I liked the best. The attention I got from handing out large sums of money was something I really enjoyed. I was finally popular. I did not worry about the consequences. I was starting to be able to hang out with the "in" crowd. This was the crowd that no one messed with in school. They were the cool kids. Now nobody was making fun of me. No one picked on me. I had control. Or so I thought.

The middle school principal eventually got word that I was handing out money all the time. I was called to the main office and told to go sit in the principal's office. By now I was used to being called to his office.

I'd been there many times in both elementary school and in middle school for stealing from other kids and for acting out in class.

The principal wanted to know what was going on. I didn't say a word. I denied everything, but he knew I was lying. He said that he'd have to call my parents, then he sent me back to class. He also said that any more issues with money would result in detention and some pretty serious consequences.

That day seemed to go by really fast. I was scared to death to go home. How was I going to explain this one? My behavior was getting worse and even I knew I wasn't going to get out of this one scot free. I walked home very slowly. I even thought about running away again so I wouldn't have to face Dad and Suzanne when I got home.

I was standing in the kitchen that night when Dad and Suzanne confronted me about the money. My dad walked into the kitchen holding the cigar box. He just looked at me and it was clear he wasn't happy. My heart sunk and I felt my whole body starting to shake a little. I heard loud stern voices from both Dad and Suzanne expressing both disappointment and utter frustration. I was told to go to my room and stay there. I started to walk there quickly and thought I'd gotten off pretty easily. But Dad trailed me, following close behind. Then I felt something hit my leg. Apparently he'd kicked me in the back of the leg out of frustration.

I started to cry. I yelled to Suzanne to keep him away from me. I screamed, "I'm sorry" as loud as I could. As I was pleading with them, my dad hit the wall with his fist. I had never seen him like this. I had seen him bitterly disappointed. I had seen him look at me with despair in his eyes. But I'd never seen him hit anything. I'd never seen him be violent at all. I was terrified. Suzanne told him to leave me alone and for him to go to their bedroom to calm down. I went to my room, where I cowered in the corner, holding my head in my arms. Then I started to cry like I had never cried before. The game was up.

Flashbacks of my mistreatment as a small child came flooding back. Events I hadn't remembered for years now hit me like a brick. They were all back — the brutality, the screaming, the crying, the desperation, the total isolation, the detachment. My heart started to race and I began to shake. I did not know what was going to happen to me next. I was expecting to be whipped with a belt, hit with a fist, or beaten really badly, because when I got punished when I was little and still living with my mom, that was what continually happened. To my relief, however, I wasn't beaten at all. I was just left alone for the rest of the night and made to stay in my room. That night, after eating dinner in my room, I made up my mind that Dad and Suzanne must be so disappointed in me that they couldn't possibly still care about me or even want me there.

For a split second, with anger overtaking me, I thought about getting the pocket knife I'd hidden in my room and threatening Dad and Suzanne with it. I thought hurting Dad and Suzanne would result in them finding a new home for me and thus be a way out of the constant day to day life of chores and responsibilities that I hated so much. I'd also be able to release the anger that had built up inside me. I'd be able to stop feeling hurt and frustrated over the fact I didn't feel anyone seemed to care about me. I wanted Dad and Suzanne to experience the hurt and pain that I felt inside as well as the loneliness that continued to fester.

That idea quickly faded as I realized that, no matter what happened, I could not bring myself to do that. Both of them had tried really hard to be my parents and to shower me with love and affection. I just didn't want any of it. I no longer felt any connection to them. I felt nothing. I didn't want them, either of them. I no longer felt any affection for them or any attachment whatsoever. I felt completely detached.

I started to make small little cuts on my arms with anything sharp I could find. I used metal from pencil erasers. I used knives and broken pieces of plastic or glass. This was now my new way to release my anger. This was a new way for me to feel any kind of emotion.

When I cut myself I did not feel the cold blade or sharp edge slicing through my skin. I didn't feel the sting of the air hitting my open skin. Instead, I felt a rush of emotion and instant relief. The anger I felt inside seemed to flow out of the open wound like a bad infection leaving my body. I'd watch as the blood slowly trickled out of my arms. At that point, due to the overwhelming amount of pain and loss I'd gone through my entire life, my emotions were almost nonexistent. Usually I cut myself in places on my body Dad and Suzanne would never see. I did not cut myself because I wanted to die. I cut myself because I just wanted to finally feel some kind of relief. Any kind.

The next day at school I went to my first period music class as usual, where I played my trumpet. My music teacher Ron noticed that there was just something not right with me that day. At the end of class he told me to stay after class to talk to him. I explained what had happened the night before. I told him that I'd stolen money from my parents and that they'd found out about it. Then I told him my dad kicked me on the back of my leg out of frustration. I pleaded with Ron not to tell anyone because I was just petrified of what my father would say or do if he found out I'd told someone. I didn't want him to get in trouble. After all, I was the one who'd created the problem. I was the one who'd made him mad. If anything, I deserved to be kicked.

Ron said that he wouldn't tell anyone and I believed him. I thanked him and walked to my next class. After school I walked home as usual. Suzanne had gone out of town to teach a travel class that day and would be spending the night away somewhere. My dad was still at work. So I let myself in with the house key that was now hidden outside in a new spot just in case we got locked out. I then went to my room and started reading my books.

Soon there was a knock at the front door. I wondered who it was. I answered the door even though Dad and Suzanne had always told me not to answer the door when I was home alone. There were two men standing there. One was wearing a police uniform. The other was wearing a suit. They introduced themselves and asked me my name. I didn't let them in, but we talked at the door. When they realized I was home alone they gave me their business cards, told me to give them to my dad, and for him to call them when he got home. Then they asked me to show them where I'd been kicked. I was upset to learn that my music teacher Ron had lied to me about telling anyone about what I'd told him. I showed them my left leg, but as I hadn't been kicked that hard, there was no bruise or mark. Then they left. Now I was really scared. I'd have to talk to my dad and tell him to call the police about what had happened.

That night when Dad got home he called the police and they came to talk to us. They questioned me at length about what had happened the night before. I told them my dad had kicked me on the back of the leg. They asked me again to show them where. I showed them the back of my right leg by mistake. I couldn't remember which leg it had been. Both men left shortly after that. Apparently they thought I'd either made up the whole story or I'd really exaggerated it. I then went straight to my room and closed the door. I didn't care to see dad's reaction after that. Things were going downhill fast.

A few days went by and it was quiet around the house. The mood was definitely different. I got up early in the morning and left for school before Dad and Suzanne got up. I did not want to see them or talk to them at this point. I figured the less I saw of them and had to talk to them, the better off we'd all be.

At school a police detective met with me to see how I was doing and to make sure everything had settled down at home. By now the school office knew I was having serious problems at home because I was making frequent trips to the counseling office to see my counselor.

One day I pretty much decided that I'd had enough. I hated doing chores and didn't want to do any of them any more. I hated the fact that people were trying to control my life and tell me what to do. So instead of walking home, I went to a friend's house with the intention of running away. I barely knew this new friend and we'd really only become friends because I'd given him some money in the past in order to gain his friendship. I didn't intend to go back home because I didn't want to be at the Hogsetts any more. Anything was better than that place.

The police came later that night to my friend's house because his mother was concerned and she'd called them. I was taken home in a police car. Dad and Suzanne seemed glad to see me. I still did not care. In fact I'd even left a note for Dad and Suzanne that morning before I went to school saying I was running away because I didn't want to do any chores. I'd been made to set the table for dinner, clean my room, and sometimes do some of the dishes or mow the lawn. The police concluded Dad and Suzanne weren't doing anything wrong and gave them some suggestions on how to help me.

About a week or so later Dad and Suzanne drove me to the local police station to talk to a detective about my behavior. The cutting, lying, stealing, and constant acting out were getting badly out of hand. They thought that if I could talk to a detective, that maybe something might just sink in to make me change. Maybe they could scare me into changing. I remember the detective well. He was around five foot ten, with mid-length neatly combed back hair. He wore a nice looking dress shirt and fancy black pants. I noticed the gun he was carrying in a shoulder holster. He sat alone with me in a room. He really drilled me about my misbehavior. He was right in my face and to the point. If at any point in the conversation he felt I was not paying attention, he sure let me know by edging closer to my face in order to get my full attention.

He said if I kept on with my current acting out behaviors like stealing, lying, self mutilating and such, that I'd end up in a local hospital. There I'd be strapped to a bed for three days to keep me safe from myself and so they could monitor my behavior. But I still really did not care. I smiled and laughed at him. Nothing he told me phased me in the least. That really upset him. I think he knew that this confrontation was not working. Our meeting was over a short while later. I went back out to the lobby and Dad and Suzanne drove me home.

I had been taught stealing was wrong, but I just didn't care. Nor did I really care about what the consequences might be for anything I did. At this point I felt that no matter what anyone said or did to me, that I wasn't going to change anything I was doing. It seemed no one was really listening to me. I felt my life was spiraling downhill and that my hope for the kind of life I wanted was quickly fading away. I wanted a life free of chores, free of homework, free of having to do anything I didn't want to do. I wanted a life where I felt people understood me. I wanted a life where I felt loved and not judged. I did not feel like I had any identity, any friends, or any family. I was alone in my own little world of aggression and manipulation. I held onto those feelings and behaviors in order to have control over my life. Only having control made me feel safe.

After the meeting with the policeman my acting out got even worse. I became obsessed with knives. I also became obsessed with suicide. I took books out of the library about knives, guns and death. It was all I could think about. I hid knives in my room. What better way to scare Dad and Suzanne? With the sharp knives, lighters and matches they knew I had, they were worried I could hurt or even kill them. These were items I'd stolen from stores, from my friends' houses, and from what I found around our house. They were also worried I could kill myself and they felt they were powerless to stop me. They were at wit's end. They concluded they could no longer trust me in the house. They were afraid for their own lives and mine.

They were worried about my self-destructive behavior, worried that I'd continue to find sharp objects to cut and hurt myself with, or worse. My self-mutilation was getting worse too. They seemed afraid I could actually die. Nothing was safe in the house because I had hidden so many would-be weapons there. Dad and Suzanne hid all their kitchen knives. No problem. I'd bring other knives home. When they confiscated my matches, I found more matches to bring home. I enjoyed being able to do anything I wanted anytime I wanted to. Dad and Suzanne had no control over me whatsoever. I did not let them. I loved it because now I was unpredictable. They had no idea what I could do, no idea who I could do it to, no idea where or when something destructive, something just awful, could happen. I was scary to them. That made me powerful. In essence, I was now in absolute total control. I was 13 years old and the world was mine!

One day, in the spring of 1993, still at age 13, I found their car keys laying on the kitchen counter. Why not go for a joy ride in their Volkswagen camper van? I put the keys in the ignition, turned on the engine, put the van in gear, and rolled backwards down the driveway. Then I got scared and went back into the house. I carefully returned the keys to the kitchen counter. No one would ever know, or so I thought. But who could explain why the van was now parked at the bottom of the driveway?

7 Another one-way journey

Dad and Suzanne were now frantic. The temporary solution they came up with was to set up a tent for me in the backyard with a portable camping toilet, sleeping bag, air mattress, a bag of books and games, and an ice chest full of snacks and drinks. This was to keep me from entering the house and finding something to hurt myself or them with. This was also to keep me from burning the house down.

They even called all my friends' parents to advise them to hide any sharp objects if I were coming over. They called my school counselor too. I was allowed in the house, supervised of course, to take showers, to change clothes, and for meals. When I showered, Dad or Suzanne stood just outside to make sure I was not hurting myself in the bathroom.

The tent became my new home. At that moment, when I first saw the tent and the ice chest, I felt terribly rejected and very very depressed. But at the same time, I was relieved. I could now make my own decisions and I could come and go as I pleased. And I didn't have to do any chores. At age 13 it was about time. Dad and Suzanne made sure the front door was locked at all times and they moved the hidden front door key to some-place where I couldn't find it.

I was in my own little world. The old world was no longer reality and, to say the least, I really did not care. I enjoyed the defiance. I enjoyed my freedom. One day in broad daylight I went around the house to the driveway out in front, unzipped my pants and peed in a straight stream all over the driveway. Suzanne came out as I was finishing. She was shocked. This, for her, was apparently the last straw.

Up to this point I had been getting intense mental health counseling for three years, starting at age 10. My psychiatrist was a wonderful man. He was very warm, friendly, and easy to talk to. He was also easy to fool, easy to manipulate. When I had my sessions with him, all I had to do was act like everything was OK. I couldn't understand how this man could possibly have any idea what I was going through. I was the one living this life, not him. I was the one who had suffered early abuse, not him. And I sure as heck did not know him, so I was not about to talk to him about anything bothering me. In fact, the less he knew about me the better.

When I met with him, usually twice a week, I stayed completely quiet and shut off about what was going on at home and elsewhere in my life. Instead of talking we played with toys he had in his office. We played doctor with a play stethoscope. We acted like we were shooting each other with toys that looked like guns. To me, I had a play date twice a week. However, when he held progress meetings with Dad and Suzanne, he was shocked about the behaviors they told him I was acting out at home. He had no idea I was even cutting myself on a regular basis. He was just another person to fool. And fool him I did.

After a few days living in my "tent city" and coming and going as I pleased, Dad and Suzanne came out and told me that we were going for a ride. They said they had called and talked with my social worker Hale. He'd told them he'd help them get me the help I needed as long as they agreed to follow the plan he'd devised for me. Everything Dad and Suzanne had tried to get me to turn my life around had failed. Everyone felt we needed to explore other options and we needed to do that immediately. I was curious to see where we were going and I had a lot of uncertainty about what Dad and Suzanne had talked to Hale about. I noticed a small suitcase I used when we traveled was also in the van. But, as usual, I said nothing.

I soon found out that the things in store for me would give me a sense of déjà vu. We drove for a while. I didn't ask any questions. I'd always been silent in the car when riding with them. Today was no different. I didn't recognize anything out the car window and I didn't care to ask. I felt the less I said the better. We finally pulled up to a building and parked. For some reason the place looked a little familiar. I was not sure when I had been there before or what it was. I just knew that I'd seen it before.

As we walked into the building I knew immediately where we were. It hit me hard. This was the same children's shelter I'd lived in before becoming a foster child. This was where my sister and I had been dropped off and abandoned by my mother Leanne eight years earlier. Old memories came flooding back. I knew what had happened then, so I had a good idea what was going to happen now. Everything at the shelter looked the same as it had eight years before. Even the pool table I'd had fun with was still there. I had an idea Dad and Suzanne were about to leave me there too and that I was going to stay there. That's exactly what had happened eight years earlier with my mother Leanne.

I don't recall what Dad and Suzanne told me before they left the shelter. They may have told me I was there temporarily to get the help I needed. They now tell me that as they left, they saw me looking back at them through a window. It looked as if my demeanor had changed. I looked relieved. I looked like all the stress I had pent up in my body all those years had been let out. As I look back on that day, I think they are right. I felt a real sense of relief. I no longer needed to feel I had an obligation to be attached to anyone. I no longer had to try to change who I was in order to conform to someone else's wishes. I felt at ease in this environment because no one knew who I was. I felt free.

Yet on the flip side, I was very sad. Part of me honestly cared for the Hogsetts. Part of me wished I could just have opened up and told them all these years everything that was on my mind, both good and bad. But that was just a thought. I could never have brought myself to do that. I did not know how. I did not know what words to use to describe the way I'd felt. I did not know how to express my feelings, any of them.

I was led into the cafeteria to a table, where I sat alone. I could not help but feel I'd been abandoned yet again. I wondered when I'd finally have some good luck in my life. I kept my head down, cautiously peering out of the corner of my eye at the few other kids and workers in the cafeteria. I was frightened and very nervous about this place. After all, my only other memory of it was a bad one. My mother Leanne had left me there, the mother who promised me the world, the mother who delivered on none of those promises, the mother who gave up on, then abandoned an innocent five-year-old boy.

I thought about my sister and wondered if she even knew where I was. Were we now lost to each other forever? I missed her so much. I knew she'd been adopted by a family near San Diego that really loved and cared for her. I wanted to talk to her. I wanted to see her. I really needed her. She was the only true connection I had left to my real family.

At this point I no longer thought Leanne was going to come back to get me. Eight years had passed and that never happened. Reality had hit me hard. I had accepted the fact that Leanne didn't want me. I had accepted the fact that she was probably gone from my life forever. I had accepted the fact that, in all probability, I would never see her again. I would probably never even learn where she'd gone or what had become of her.

I was not sure what to expect, how long I was going to be in this shelter, or where I'd be going next. I thought to myself, "Whatever. My life just could not get any worse." Right then and there I just gave up. I now knew with certainty that I had no hope of a happy life. After all, everyone I had gotten close to, or at least tried to get close to, had given up on me and tossed me aside. I was a throwaway. Why should I have expected anything better?

I was led to one of the doors that lined the circular walkway. Inside was a room with a row of beds with lockers between them lining one side of the wall and another row of beds with lockers lining the other side of the wall. There was a common room to the right and a bathroom to the left. There were two tall black men and at least twelve teenaged boys inside the room. They all stared at me when I came in. The teens all looked older than me. They looked stronger and meaner than me too.

I was afraid for a while until the two men came over and introduced themselves. Their names were Van and Christian. They were the staff in charge of the dorm that day. They were smiling and immediately made me feel comfortable. The boys soon came over and started to introduce themselves. A few even patted me on the back and shook my hand. After all, they were really no different than me. They were also just kids living in a shelter because no one wanted them.

I put the things they provided (shampoo, toothbrush, toothpaste, comb and soap) away in my locker, unpacked my small suitcase, and made up my bed. Then I sat down with Van, who explained the shelter and dorm rules. Life at the shelter actually wasn't all that bad. I began to learn the rules and the ropes and I fit in well with the other boys. These boys liked me for who I was. They didn't know much about me and I didn't have to give them money or anything else to get them to like me.

I attended an on-site school and did very well in my classes. Every month the school had an award ceremony for the students who were doing well. We usually went to a restaurant to eat and the staff passed out awards. The awards were trophies and I earned one every time we held the monthly meeting and award ceremony. Some said, "Outstanding Student." Others said, "Most Progress," and "Honor Roll." Even the shelter staff members were amazed at my ability in school. It really felt good to get that kind of recognition. I felt very much at ease there because there was no one I had to confide in and no one I had to feel close to. No one there knew my background, and no one expected me to behave a certain way. I did have to follow the shelter rules, but they were quite lax.

One day turned out to be a bad day for me however. I woke up that morning with a small headache and not feeling well. I went to class as usual. Around lunchtime I asked to go back to the dorm because I still didn't feel well. I was allowed to and my school teacher called the nurse's station to let them know. As I walked to the dorm a sudden massive pain surged through my head. It felt like something was pushing down on my skull. It hurt so badly I fell to the ground and began to scream. I tried to get up, but every time I did, it felt as if there were a force pushing me back to the ground.

The nurse came running out of the shelter with a wheelchair. She wheeled me into the nurses' station and on into a room with a bed. She helped me onto the bed and began to assess my condition by taking my vital signs and asking me questions. She gave me some Tylenol and let me lay there for a while. When I began to feel better I went back to the dorm.

That night my head began to hurt again. My eyes were not focusing and I began to have double vision. The nurse came and took me back to the nurses' station. Once again I lay in the bed. She gave me another Tylenol and after about an hour she turned the TV on for me. About five minutes after starting to watch TV I began to shake and flail my arms in all directions, unable to control what was happening to me. Then I began to throw up over the side of the bed. The nurse came running in, turned off the TV, and held my arms. She applied a cold washrag to my head and I soon fell asleep. I later realized I'd had a grand mal epileptic seizure.

The next day my father came. The shelter staff had called him and told him what had happened. He came to take me to the doctor's office to have me examined. I was taken to see the pediatric neurologist I'd seen since infancy. I thought maybe I was having this awful pain due to my hydrocephalus and the shunt. The doctor performed a CT scan, which showed that nothing was wrong with my shunt. He said it sounded more like a migraine headache. I'd had those before, but nothing like this.

On the way back to the shelter my father said he did not believe that I was going through that much pain and that I was exaggerating. After all, the doctor had said that I just had a bad headache. I told him I was not lying and that I did not care what he thought. I was really angry with him. I was going through some massive episode of extreme pain and my own father had the nerve to doubt me! I was so mad that I didn't talk to him the rest of the way back to the shelter. When he dropped me off and walked me inside I didn't even say goodbye to him. I couldn't have cared less at that point. The head pain lasted a few more days but it was less intense than it had been. I was really glad when those episodes were over.

I was getting used to shelter life and it wasn't all that bad. Soon I found out that a new children's shelter was going to be built to house and help more kids and that this one was going to be closed down. I, along with three other kids from the shelter, was selected to sing at the groundbreaking ceremony for the new shelter. It was an experience like no other. The three kids and I who were chosen to sing appeared on TV and were written about in local newspaper articles. I could not believe it. It was so cool. We performed on a stage outside. Hundreds of people came, including news people. Even Dad and Suzanne came and were excited to see me perform.

I spent close to three months at the shelter. While I was there I attended my first major league baseball game at Oakland Stadium. I made new friends. I felt needed and wanted. I felt like I had a place where for once people understood me. I was the happiest I'd been in a very long time.

Part Three

On the road to attachment — transformation

8   Intensive treatment

I learned that I'd be leaving the shelter but I wasn't going home. Instead, I was told I was going to a place to get treatment, whatever that meant. It was described to me as a place that specialized in helping teens with behavior like mine. I did not know where this place was or when I'd be going. But I was excited about going and glad in a way that I wasn't going back home.

Near the end of my shelter stay my father came and picked me up again. This time we drove four and a half hours north to Chico, California, to meet with a representative of the facility where I'd possibly be going. The representative asked me a few questions. One question was, "How would you feel if, once you arrived at the facility, you could not have contact with any family members for the first 30 days?" I said, "I think that's bullshit." I pretended to act like a macho big shot. After the interview my dad drove me back to the shelter and dropped me off.

A few days later I learned that I'd been accepted by this facility, a mental health treatment center in Redding, California, about 260 miles north of the San Jose shelter. I was told I'd be staying there for at least six months and that my treatment would be carried out in a group home setting. My social worker Hale came one morning and drove me all the way there.

There are different classifications for childrens' group homes, ranging from level 9 (the lowest level) to level 14 (the highest level). The levels reflect the intensity of treatment the child needs. Kids can move from a higher level of care to a lower level of care and vice versa, depending on the progress they make dealing with their problems. If they start to show signs of more aggressive negative behavior, they may be transferred to a higher level facility. Likewise, if they show growth and take steps in the right direction, they can be transferred to a lower level group home or even go home.

When a child arrives at a group home there is a transition period commonly referred to as the honeymoon phase. In this phase the child usually is very careful not to display any mental health issues. The aggression, defiance, self harm or other behaviors that may have contributed to their referral to the home in the first place are usually kept in check by the child. This is the time when the child gets to know how the home operates and gets acquainted with the other children and staff there. The child is unfamiliar with the new environment and may be very nervous about his or her new situation.

The honeymoon phase can last a few days or a few weeks. The medical conditions the child has been diagnosed with or behavior he or she has exhibited determine the level of care needed in order for that child to succeed with his or her treatment. The more aggressive and emotionally disturbed the child is, the more likely the child will be placed in a higher level of care, or even the highest level, level 14.

A child may be placed in a group home by Social Services, the Probation Department, or privately. Every child has a treatment plan that is devised when first coming, or even before coming to the home. It outlines both short and long term goals and the course of treatment needed. It also defines the length of stay at the home. The average stay is around six months. This of course can change depending on the progress the child has made.

The group home I was assigned to was located just outside Redding and was operated by an organization called Victor Youth Services. It was a level 14 home for severely emotionally disturbed kids. Victor operated private group homes licensed by the State of California. For me, coming to Victor was the beginning of a battle that I thought I'd never win.

I did not want to leave the shelter, as I had begun to bond with the other kids and the staff. I was starting to feel comfortable there. I felt I was never judged by anyone there. But now, again, I had no choice. I was forced to move again and start this new phase of my life. As we drove to Redding all kinds of ideas came to mind about what to expect. I wondered what the other kids were going to be like. I wondered what the staff was going to be like. I had never heard of group homes before and I wondered if they were like jail. I was nervous. I was also afraid the other kids might hurt me.

The drive must have taken at least five hours. We stopped at a diner along the way so we could get something to eat. The ride was a quiet one. Most of the time I just sat looking at the trees and the sky as we drove. I could not help but think of all the people I had left behind at the shelter. I couldn't help but think of Dad and Suzanne and my friends at home. I wondered if I'd ever see any of them again. I thought of my sister Julia, who was still living in Southern California. I wondered when I'd see her again and how to let her know where I was now. I'd had regular visits with her while living at Dad and Suzanne's. But now I was unsure about everything. I eventually fell asleep in the car and woke up only when Hale said we'd arrived.

OK, I thought, here we go. I got out of the car. The first thing I noticed was that it was really hot! I had never been able to deal with the heat very well. (When I got overheated I got headaches, vomited, and tired easily.) I walked into a small office and sat down. I didn't bring many belongings with me, only the clothes I was wearing and a small backpack with a few things I had brought from the children's shelter. A few grownups came out and were introduced to us including a woman named Mary. She said she'd be driving me to the house where I'd be staying. As she helped me with my things, I turned around and hugged Hale, and Mary and I were off.

I sat in Mary's car thinking about how I had ended up here. I wondered if I had just changed something in my behavior and proven to Dad and Suzanne I could change, if I'd still be here. I wondered what the home was going to be like and what the other kids would be like. I was unsure how I was going to cope with being so far from home and so far from the day to day life I was used to at the shelter.

It seemed like we drove forever. We drove through shopping areas, residential areas, got onto a freeway and got off in what looked like a different city. There was a small gas station to the left, and as we went right I saw nothing but rolling hills with trees and a few houses. We also passed a golf course. We turned right and continued driving for at least another five minutes. Then we turned left onto a quiet residential street, Queens Way. About three houses down Queens Way we pulled into a driveway. We had arrived at the group home where I was going to be staying.

I just looked at the house and the surrounding area in amazement. I could not believe that I was actually here at the group home. I knew I could not run away because this whole area was completely new to me and I'd have absolutely no idea where to go. I thought I'd just have to prepare myself for whatever would greet me at the door.

Mary took me inside and led me down a hallway to the left of the front door. I noticed there were rooms to the right and left with two beds in each. She then led me to a room all the way in the back. There were also two beds in this room and it even had its own bathroom. I thought that was very cool. I'd never had my own bathroom before.

Mary showed me which bed was mine, then helped me put away my few belongings. She must have known I was coming that day because everything I needed was spread out neatly on my bed — shampoo, conditioner, soap, a comb, a toothbrush and toothpaste. There was even aftershave. Even though I didn't have much to shave at age 13, I shaved anyway because I wanted to appear older and tougher that I really was. I quickly put all the toiletries away in a drawer under my bed.

Then Mary took me on a tour of the home. Along the hallway was another bathroom and an office. This was the office that the house staff used for everything from storing medications to paperwork. Straight ahead, at the end of the hallway, was the family room, which had a pool table. I thought the pool table was really neat and was excited that one day soon I might be able to play pool there. Just past the pool table, as you stepped up to another level, there was a picnic table and benches. This was where we'd be eating our house meals. It was a good sized house. I began to feel a little more comfortable at that moment. Mary then got to work making lunch for everyone for the next day. I was told that the other boys were out on a day trip and would be returning soon.

The home I was assigned to housed only teenaged boys. I was the youngest boy there. I was still 13. The other boys were 14 to 18 years old. There were other homes that housed only girls. There was room for six kids in each home, with two kids to a room. There were 10 homes in all run by Victor Youth Services.

I sat in the living room and talked to Mary while she was making lunch. The other boys soon arrived and when they opened the door I was taken aback. They were very loud and very hyper. This frightened me. These boys seemed to be a lot different from anyone I'd ever known. They were bigger and meaner looking. I was neither loud nor hyper and I didn't understand why these kids were. I wanted to get out of there right away. I wanted to run as far away as I could get and never look back. This clearly was not the right place for me.

Even though the house could accommodate six, when I arrived there were only four boys and me there. The four were Bruce, Moses, Chris and Juan. Bruce was a big kid, tall and fat. He smiled as he came through the door. He was the one who seemed the most hyper. I thought that I'd better watch myself around him because he intimidated me. I was a bit afraid of him.

Moses was tall and thin and seemed to slump over as he walked. He also seemed a little slow in his movements. I felt calm when I saw him because I did not see him as a threat. That was nice. Chris had a medium build and seemed a little older than the other boys. He had red hair and crooked teeth. He looked like he wasn't like the other kids. He seemed like someone who I'd want to hang around with. He looked easy-going, quiet, and to be a go-with-the-flow kind of person.

Then there was Juan. He immediately made me very nervous. He was short and his black hair was pulled back into a ponytail. He had a moustache, a goatee, and a noticeable acne problem. But what really concerned me was that he looked just like the gang members I'd seen so often on TV. He wore a white tank top that he tucked into long shorts that sagged off his hips. He wore long white socks that he pulled all the way up so his shorts covered them. Black house slippers finished off his outfit. I also noticed that he had a lot of muscle. His arms and chest were huge! I was only thirteen and had never seen anyone dress like that. I'd developed a stereotype of people by watching TV and listening to the news. Gangs really frightened me and anyone resembling a gang member really made my heart race!

The boys introduced themselves to me one by one. They all welcomed me to the house and even smiled when they did. Every time they came over I took a step back and became guarded. Even though they seemed welcoming, I still knew nothing about them. I had no idea who these boys were, what they were like, what their intentions were, or even what issues they had which caused them to come to the group home in the first place.

Bruce immediately started asking me questions about who I was and why was I there. It felt like he was prying into my personal business. That made me really leery of him and I started to get upset. But I kept that inside because I didn't know anything about anyone there and I didn't want to start trouble on my first day in the house.

After the introductions I went to my room. Moses was my roommate. The other boys seemed to follow me wherever I went. This seemed to go on for days. It was really annoying but I just dealt with it and pretended it did not bother me. I gave the other boys some of the few possessions I'd brought from the shelter in the hope of starting things off on the right foot. Whether that mattered to them or not, I did not know. But since it had worked before, why not try it again?

Later that day Mary took me to a store to buy some much needed clothes. I hadn't brought much with me. And as I was growing by leaps and bounds, I outgrew pretty much everything within a month or so. I picked out a few pair of pants, a couple shirts, some underwear, socks, and a belt. I was very grateful for the new clothes. I was really happy to know someone was looking out for me.

Later that night Moses and I learned a little about each other. We both enjoyed listening to the same music, like Metallica, Aerosmith and other heavy metal bands. We also liked to play chess. He pulled out his chess board from under his bed and we played two games. I won one and so did he. More important to me though was the fact that I shared a room with someone who had many of the same interests and ideas that I had. This helped me relax and let my guard down a little for the first night I was there.

After we finished playing chess we got ready for bed. I didn't get under the covers at all that night. I was still slightly worried. If someone were to try to bother or attack me that night, I wanted to be able to react and defend myself fast enough. I felt the covers would get in my way. So I slept on top of the covers and covered myself loosely with an extra blanket. I lay there that night thinking about so many things that had happened in my life. I hoped that I'd wake up the next morning away from this unfamiliar house. I hoped I would wake up in a place where everything was perfect. To me the perfect place was somewhere I would be valued and listened to, where I would be loved unconditionally, where I would fit in and feel like I belonged to a true family. I turned over and a few tears rolled down my cheek before I finally fell asleep.

Because my behavior had been out of control (stealing, lying, self mutilation, defiance, anger and more), I'd been sent to a level 14 home. Level 14 facilities were considered "hands-on." That meant that if a child got out of control and posed a danger to himself or others, the group home staff members were authorized to restrain him or her. Only staff trained in restraint procedures could restrain the child. This involved at least two staff members. Each held down one arm and one leg of the child in order to prevent any further escalation of any incident. A third staff member was always there as a witness to make sure the restraint was performed properly and that the child was not in danger of being hurt. The length of time the child was held down depended solely on how fast he or she calmed down.

As the child calmed down, the staff released either one arm or one leg. If the child stayed calm, another arm or leg would be released. Usually if one arm was released, then a leg would be released. Both legs were never released at the same time. Both arms were never released at the same time either. This restraint usually worked, as it allowed the child to scream, yell, curse and exert so much energy that sooner or later he or she would be too exhausted to continue the bad behavior. Most importantly, the child and everyone else in the house would stay safe.

In the end, this group home experience would prove to be one of the most difficult, but also one of the best things that I ever underwent. It helped me transform my life. We've all heard the expression, "Well, I am this way because of the way that I was raised." While this may be true to some extent, in the end, it's our own decision whether or not to break the cycle of abuse and neglect and become the person we want to become. My belief that I was just a victim of my upbringing served as my crutch for many years. That was also my excuse for my bad behavior in the group home for quite some time.

In the beginning, I went through my honeymoon phase, which probably lasted just a week or so. But then the real me came out. Or what I thought was the real me. It started with an incident with another resident. As I mentioned earlier, Bruce was one of the boys I was leery of. He was the one who was bigger than I was, the one I really decided I didn't want to upset or get into a fight with.

I tried my best for the first week to steer clear and not upset him, but it seemed that he wanted a confrontation. He was someone who, no matter what I said to him, no matter how nice I was, seemed to feel the need to push my buttons. He was loud and very hyper. He always seemed to like to go into my room, which was not allowed. He stole the belongings that I cared the most about, then denied he did anything wrong. It almost sounded like something I'd done so often at home. I was very annoyed about this. I felt violated. It seemed the staff members were not doing anything about it that worked. No matter what they told Bruce, he kept doing this.

What few things I had needed to be protected. They were mine and other people needed to keep their hands off them. If they did not want to listen, then I'd have to stand up for myself. And that is exactly what I did. I went over to Bruce and with all my might pushed him against the wall. He fell against it, then hit the floor. As he fell, I started to scream at him. I cursed at him, telling him that I wanted him to stop messing with my stuff. He got back up off the floor and pushed me back really hard. I landed halfway down the hall. At this point a staff member ran over and quickly separated us. And true to form, I was the one who got in trouble. The only one. Boy was I mad! I did not understand why I got in trouble and Bruce, the instigator, did not. All I was doing was standing up for myself.

I was sent to my room to calm down. I went reluctantly, cursing out loud all the way. A short time later a staff member came in, talked to me, and apologized for Bruce's behavior. But he also reprimanded me for taking matters into my own hands. Even though I acted as if I understood, I refused to listen to that. Just then my anger came to a boiling point. I thought that if this was what group home life was going to be like, then I was going to be a force to be reckoned with. I was determined to show my true colors and rebel against anything that got in my way.

Bruce and I were separated from each other for the rest of the day. But even though we were separated, he still looked at me and snickered with a half-cocked smile on his face. I just wanted to go over to him and punch his nose in, right through his ugly face. But with staff next to him at all times, there was no way I could get to him.

Chris, on the other hand, was someone I could start to bond with right away. He saw me as a little brother in a way. He was the one who stood up for me when I could not stand up for myself. He offered me advice on how to deal with certain situations. He tried to teach me how to control my anger and to let the small things I couldn't control just roll off my shoulders. I learned that he was going to graduate soon from the program since he was doing so well. I listened intently to him and trusted him to a point. To a point because I didn't feel I could really trust anybody. But it was reassuring to know that someone would protect me if need be.

Juan made me constantly feel on edge because he looked just like a gang member. He flaunted certain mannerisms around the house, making different signs with his hands that I'd later find out were gang gestures. He constantly prayed to God and asked me to join in. But I always turned him down, as I'd never really felt comfortable praying. Juan was later discharged from the home because he wasn't making any progress. I didn't know where he went and at the time I really didn't care. I was just glad he was gone. It was as if a big weight had been lifted off my chest and I could breathe just a little easier.

I went to middle school while at Victor, at an alternative school called Live Oak. Live Oak was for kids who were not quite ready for public school because they acted out a lot. I even saw a few kids there who I remembered from the San Jose children's shelter. The class sizes were small, about 15 kids per class, so I got plenty of individual help and attention from the teachers. I even earned the Principal's Award for outstanding achievement and grades. I did very well academically and earned my first straight A report card. I could not wait to show everyone.

Because I was doing so well, after I finished eighth grade at Live Oak, I was transferred to Central Valley High School. I started my freshman year, ninth grade, there. Central Valley was a public school that so-called normal kids went to. And there were a lot of kids. The first day I was dropped off at school in the group home van. I got out and was immediately besieged by other kids questioning me. They wanted to know if I lived in a group home. I did not answer. Instead, I just held my head down. I felt very much out of place. This was high school, a completely new world to me. I was not sure how to act or how to fit in.

Dad and Suzanne brought my trumpet to the group home and I went to music class at the high school. That made me happy. But as I hadn't played the trumpet for a while, I was not as good at it as I used to be. This was a big let down for me, as music had been one of my passions.

I joined the marching band in my new school. We played at football games and other school events. Because I felt so badly out of place, I was really miserable. One night, while performing at a football game, I got so mad at the music teacher that I threw my trumpet down on the ground and began stomping on it with my foot. When my rampage was over the trumpet was so badly damaged that I just tossed it into the trash and walked away. One of the group home staff members was there and he took the trumpet out of the trash can. But I went over, grabbed it out of his hands, threw it back on the ground, and walked off. I never went back to the music class after that. At that point I really couldn't have cared less.

Some of the other classes were not bad. I especially enjoyed my science classes. Science fascinated me because the classwork was very hands-on. Hands-on had always been the best way for me to learn. Math on the other hand was difficult for me. No matter how hard I tried to learn it, I just couldn't make sense of any of the problems. I had no interest in learning any of it. It seemed to have no relevance to my life at all. So why should I care about it? I didn't even try. To get by I made up all my own answers. It didn't matter to me at all if I got them all wrong. Part of me liked to be defiant like this because I felt it gave me control, and that I loved. At the same time another part of me was just frustrated because of having to spend so much time on something I felt I could never understand.

Central Valley High School was an open campus school. This meant that during lunch breaks we were allowed to walk off campus to go to the store or smoke or do whatever we wanted to. I'd tried puffing away on a few cigarettes back in middle school in Palo Alto. But while at the group home I started smoking on a regular basis. This was against the rules and I got in a lot of trouble over it. But that did not stop me at all from smoking at lunch. It didn't even stop me from hiding cigarettes in my groin area and sneaking them back into the group home. The staff was not allowed to check there so I knew it was the perfect place to hide things.

I also started hanging out with a group of kids at my new high school that other people would consider to be bad kids. On occasion these kids decided to skip school. They were the ones who always got in the most trouble. They were the pot smokers. Even though I did not use drugs I felt a weird sense of connection with this group. It seemed like only they understood me. Sometimes I traded cigarettes at school for small amounts of marijuana, which I then hid and took back to the group home. I gave the pot to the kids at the home who chose to indulge in it. This helped me up my status with the other boys there. The more cigarettes and pot I brought back for them from school, the less I was messed with and the more power I felt I had.

Group home life wasn't always so bad. In the back of the house there was a narrow trail that led to a small creek. We often took walks and fished or swam there, depending on the weather. In the winter we took trips to Mt. Shasta to go sledding. We took frequent trips to Shasta Lake and Whiskeytown Lake to go fishing, canoeing and camping. Outings were always planned in advance and usually took place on the weekends.

Within our house there were four achievement levels. The level you were on reflected how well you complied with the rules and worked to resolve your issues. House level one was the lowest level and level four was the highest. Level one kids had no privileges at all. Level two kids could go on basic outings, listen to music, watch TV, and stay up late. Level three kids could also go off-site by themselves for up to a half-hour. They also got more allowance money and could stay up later. Level four kids were ready to graduate from the program.

Every Monday we had a social night. All ten of the houses in the Victor group home system got together, mingled and enjoyed activities like skating, bowling, ice cream parties, swimming and much more. After spending all day every day in a house with other boys it was quite nice to see some girls. Only levels two, three and four were allowed to attend these events. But no matter what the incentives were, they did not stop me from acting out. On many occasions I had to stay back at the house while the other kids went and had fun. I'd been placed back down to level 1 so I hadn't been permitted to go.

The house also had problems with some of its staff members. Some of them allowed us to smoke, even though smoking was against the rules. Sometimes they even took us for walks and gave us cigarettes. Sometimes they even bought them for us. I loved it! Here I was in a group home and I was still allowed to break the rules without punishment. Unfortunately these lucky breaks didn't go on for long. Whenever one of us got mad at a staff member we told the house manager everything he had done wrong. This resulted in an investigation, after which the staff member involved was sometimes fired. In this setting we were master manipulators.

When we didn't succeed in getting what we wanted, we had no problem running our mouths and getting even as we called it. In a way it was fun. It was a game that never got boring. There were, however, good staff members there too. These were people who kept their composure, never let what we did or said get to them, and who never took it personally. They were there for the right reasons. They took a keen interest in what we were doing and always listened to us, no matter what mood we were in.

Not all the other boys saw them the way I came to see them. In the beginning I didn't see them so positively either. When I first came I saw them as mean, always poking their noses into my business and telling me what to do. They were strict and hardly ever let me get away with anything. They always wanted to know what I was doing and where I was going. If I did something wrong they were the first to discipline me. This usually came in the form of room time, time outs, work detail and other chores I really hated to do.

I knew what time each staff member was due at work. As soon as they arrived I immediately changed my attitude to one of a pissed off person. I did this a lot the first few months I was there. I often hoped they'd call in sick or that they'd quit. Of course I had no such luck. Two of the staff members were particularly "in my face," Jeff and Richard. Jeff was a tall skinny guy with shoulder length wavy black hair. He had a mustache and a black leopard tattoo on his right forearm. I thought that was the neatest thing I'd ever seen. I could tell from the start that he was not a pushover. I liked him because he had a way about him that was cool.

Rich was older, partly bald, with a moustache and beard. He was tall and a little husky. He reminded me of a lumberjack because he always wore plaid flannel shirts to work. He also seemed to be a bit of a father figure in the way he came across. His demeanor was one of a very confident caring man. He was the house manager, the man who made all the final decisions for the house. He was by far the strictest guy on the staff. Don't get me wrong. There were other staff members there I got along with and who were good workers and good people. But Rich and Jeff impacted me the most. They helped me change my life.

My behavior at the house got a lot worse before it got better. As I've said, my honeymoon phase was short lived. It seemed that the other kids there knew what buttons of mine to push to get a reaction. Likewise, I knew what buttons of theirs to push. I thought these little punks needed a good ass whooping. How dare they think they can just push me around? Of course, with this attitude, I was never able to form close relationships with any of the other boys. I did not understand that they too had problems that they were there to work on. I'd felt close to my roommate Moses at first, but later distanced myself from him after seeing him cut his neck and arms.

I tried to be friendly at times with some of them, but they rejected me quite often. Some of them even told me that I was annoying, that I was childish, and that I was a brat. The name calling angered me even more. They knew nothing about my past life, nothing about what I'd gone through before coming there. They knew next to nothing about me. How dare they judge me like that?

Rage and hatred were consuming me so fast that I felt like I was going to explode. The tension in the house was so thick you could just feel it everywhere. My blood was boiling. I wanted to hurt someone very badly, and I did not care who. I just wanted to release the anger that was pent up inside. I was so angry at the other kids in the house constantly picking on me, making fun of me, and trying to pick fights with me. On many occasions the group home staff did step in and tried to intervene, but no matter how hard they tried, they could not be everywhere at once. Sure there were punishments handed out to the offenders, but they weren't much of a deterrent.

I needed a quick fix, so I cut on my arms that night. I managed to take a pencil and break off the metal piece which held the eraser. In the house bathroom, with the door closed, I used that sharp end to make small cuts on my arms and stomach.

Again, I did not feel anything physically. I felt no pain at all. But I released my anger. While I was doing, this I'd mentally checked out. It was as if my body was there, but my mind was not. They were two separate entities. After about ten minutes in the bathroom I cleaned myself up and came out as if nothing had happened. Staff found out though when I took my shirt off to play basketball the next day. When questioned on the basketball court, I denied the whole thing, but there was no hiding the truth. What was done was done.

Because of the self-mutilation, I was placed on staff watch at all times. Since the house operated on a "level system" for behaviors, I was placed back down to level one, the lowest level. I had no freedoms at that point. That got me even more upset. I went into the house, slamming the door back against the wall as I walked inside. I began to punch the walls with my fist and kick them hard. I was told to stop of course, but now I was so angry I was not hearing what they were saying. All I thought about was hitting something or someone as I flew into a rage. I began to get even angrier and eventually I lost touch with reality around me. I no longer knew what was real and what was not. I had tunnel vision. I only saw anger everywhere around me. I blocked everything else out.

I went into the living room, grabbed a couple of couches and flipped them over, then threw some picture frames onto the floor, hoping they'd break. I was screaming and yelling at the top of my lungs. I sounded like a grizzly bear roaring at a predator. Then I went into the dining room and turned over the dining room table. Again I was asked to stop, change my behavior and calm down. Again I did not listen. Instead, I turned to face the staff members. Then I lunged at them with my fists clenched. When I got within inches of them I raised my fists. That was a bad idea. I was restrained immediately by two staff members, Rich and Emanuel.

Emanuel was a really big guy. I mean huge! He could probably have held me down with one hand, but that was against the rules. When I was restrained, I of course tried to squirm out of the restraint, but that did not work. I tried kicking the staff but they had a firm hold on my feet so that did not work either. I could scream and yell though. And boy did I. I must have called them every bad, dirty name, every curse word in the book. I let out low yells that then progressed to a high pitch. As I screamed at the top of my lungs I felt most of my anger and rage leave my body. Like that it was gone.

All of that anger had taken years and years to build up in me. I'd never talked to anyone about it. I'd never really unloaded much of the anger on anything or anyone. Instead, it just sat inside me, layer after layer, year after year, festering, like a geyser, just waiting to let off steam. The more emotional baggage I allowed myself to pack in, the more volatile and unstable I became. The more I thought about the anger, the more it seemed I was just ready to explode. In a way I held the anger as a power card just waiting to be played. It was a way to strike fear in other people's hearts and thereby have control over them and over almost any situation.

There was only so much pressure I could hold in before releasing it. I was full. I could no longer hold any more. The kids teasing me non-stop and upsetting me was the last straw. My anger just came pouring out like an uncontrollable volcanic eruption. No one and no thing were safe from me and there were no boundaries. I don't think I could even have stopped myself from hurting someone at that point. And it didn't matter who.

Being restrained by Rich and Emanuel that day was a good thing because it allowed me to scream and yell and vent my frustrations without further hurting myself or anyone else. Plus all of the squirming

I did while I was being held down really tired me out. By the end of the restraint, which usually lasted 20 minutes or so, I was so exhausted I fell asleep as soon as I went to bed. That was a plus for the staff.

After I'd been there for about a year, one night I decided that I'd had enough of living in the group home. It was time for me to be on my own, so I decided to run away. My roommate Moses was eager to leave too, so he went with me. The problem was that we lived out in the middle of nowhere. It was midnight and we had no flashlights. We knew where another one of the group home houses was. It was a girls' house. So we decided we'd try to walk there to see if any of the girls wanted to have some fun with us. We climbed out our window and started to walk along the road.

The moon was out and we could make out different objects along the way, so we had an idea where we were going. Anytime a car came we ducked out of the way, thinking that it was someone from the group home looking for us. We cut across fields and roads using only the moonlight to find our way. We walked for what seemed like two hours. Finally we made it to the girls' house, but that was all.

When we arrived staff from three different group homes were waiting for us. I had no idea how they knew where we were, but they grabbed us and put us in the van. I did not put up any resistance, as I was way too tired from the long walk. I apologized many times on the way back to the house. I knew what I'd done was wrong. However I did not care what the consequences for me would be. This was nothing new to me. I did what I wanted without guilt. Then, if caught, I tried to get out of the punishment by crying and saying that I was sorry and pleading to be given another chance. That never worked. I found out later that my house staff knew I possibly had a girlfriend in the girls' house, so naturally that was the first place they'd looked. Their hunch was right.

I ran away a few more times during what would turn out to be a two-year stay at Victor. I was always found, mostly because I wanted to be. I ran away because I wanted the attention. I craved any attention, good or bad. I was never worried about the consequences of my actions or how they might affect other people. But when I was punished I acted like a tyrant, hitting and breaking things because I got in trouble. And, of course, with that came restraints. I was restrained a great deal during the first six months of my stay. It seemed to happen almost every other day.

I felt so much anger and rage as a result of my past — all of the abuse, the neglect, the feeling that no one understood me, that no one cared, and losing my mother. I felt like a bad gift that keeps getting sent from place to place, the gift nobody wants to keep for long. But I had no idea how to express how I felt. I could not control my anger either. I had no impulse control. So more often than not, when I got upset, I either tried to hit a kid or staff member or I attempted to destroy the house by breaking everything I got my hands on. I'd then find myself on the floor, with staff holding me down. I'd scream, yell and try to fight with them, but they were bigger than I was, and there was no way I was going to be able to hurt them.

I was still taking the anti-seizure medication Tegretol to help control my epilepsy and headaches. It was not a psychotropic medication, a medicine to help me with my mental health issues. It just made my epileptic seizures milder and helped me have fewer headaches. I took the Tegretol twice a day. I learned later that it could also be used as a mood stabilizer. Maybe that was what the staff was hoping it would do.

A therapist named Ed also came to the house regularly. He was an older soft-spoken man, a really nice guy. He sat with me on several occasions and tried to get to the heart of what was giving me all these emotional problems. But as I'd done before, I just shut down. The wall that I'd built to protect me from and to block out pain and all the other negative emotions I felt went right up. I'd built an emotional fortress around me. I did not let anyone in for a very long time.

Talking about feelings and emotions was just not a cool thing to do. I could not trust anyone. I could not let my guard down. Not at all. I could not let anyone in to discover my innermost best kept secrets. I was not about to talk about what made me mad or what made me sad. I knew that if I did, people would only judge me and put me down. I felt that I'd then be seen as weak, unable to protect myself. No one was going to break me down and cause me to be perceived as weak.

I was afraid someone would see I might have a soft side, that someone would see I was vulnerable. Being angry and seemingly emotionless was my control. I could not let anyone see that I was hurting on the inside. The less people knew about the real me, the more powerful I felt.

When I arrived at Victor I didn't care about anyone or anything in the world. I had given up. I felt the whole world misunderstood me and that I was just a throwaway, discarded like trash by everyone I'd loved. I felt my life was useless and that no one cared about who I was or who I would become. I was enveloped in so much pain and hurt that I just wanted other people to feel what I was feeling. But soon I learned that wanting to hurt people was not the answer.

9 Reconnecting

Dad and Suzanne came to visit me at Victor. My social worker Hale came to visit me too. They all came when they could, but as it was an all-day-long drive, they couldn't come that often. It was nice when they did come. It showed me that they still cared and were wondering how I was doing. I was allowed to make phone calls to them as long as my behavior was positive and I was following the house rules. I was usually allowed one phone call a week. Dad and Suzanne brought me comics to read every time they came. I loved reading comics, especially Garfield. Anything that made me laugh, anything that let me escape reality, was great.

After spending over a year at Victor and after getting intense counseling from therapist Ed, I came to accept Dad and Suzanne as my parents. Ed helped me realize that they had always loved me and that they had always wanted me. I was soon able to think of them as my parents and to call them Mom and Dad. I would also on occasion, depending on my behavior and what level I was on, be allowed to go on home visits. These allowed me to leave Victor and travel to stay with Dad and Mom at their house for a few days at a time. I didn't think of it as my house any longer though. I felt I was not entitled to call it my house. Their house really never felt like a home to me. I felt that I really did not belong there. After being away for so long, it felt even stranger than ever being there. At Victor I was used to the other boys running around and creating chaos, so the quiet at Dad and Mom's house was eerie.

I did go on another visit while I was still at Victor. I was approved by the group home agency and my social worker to go to southern California during the Christmas holidays to stay with my sister Julia. I was so happy. I was bursting with joy and excitement. I hadn't seen Julia in more than two years. I missed her terribly.

I flew on my own from Sacramento to Los Angeles. I'd flown many times before so this was no problem for me. When I got off the plane I saw Julia and ran to her as fast as I could. I hugged her tightly. I was so happy to see her that I began to cry. She kissed me on the cheek and hugged me again. Julia had grown up. The sister who stood before me was an adorable freckled beauty, standing five feet six inches tall, with long shiny brown hair. She was just beautiful!

When we got to her house there was a big surprise. Another person was coming for the holidays, another sister. I had another sister! I could hardly believe it. My entire life I'd only known about Julia. I thought this was so amazing! I was in disbelief. My other sister's name was Jessica. She was Julia's fraternal twin. Jessica had been adopted when she was six months old and not even Julia had known about her until recently. I could not wait to meet her.

Jessica lived in Turlock, California, near Modesto. Like Julia, she was now 16 years old. She was blond with blue eyes and was about the same height as Julia. We picked her up at the bus station on Christmas eve. I felt a little awkward seeing her and talking to her. After all, what were we going to talk about? We knew nothing about each other. We talked about our interests and what we liked and disliked. We talked about our biological mother and Jessica's dad. Julia, Jessica and I had the same biological mother but I had a different biological father than they did. Julia and Jessica were my half sisters. But in my eyes, half, whole, it was all the same. I just could not get over the fact that I had another sister. I had always thought that Julia was the only family I still had.

We ended up taking a trip to Disneyland while Jessica was there visiting. It was terrific. I was finally getting to know my real family, including a sister I never even knew I had. Disneyland was the perfect place to share that joy. It was one of the best days of my life. I flew back to Sacramento with a good feeling in my gut and nothing but good memories, memories that would last a lifetime. I had so much to talk about to Jeff. I could not wait to tell him.

I was never one to start any problems in the group home. Or at least that was what I thought. Generally my acting out happened when other kids made me really mad or when I received punishment I considered unfair. Sometimes however I just craved any kind of attention I could get, so I interjected myself into someone else's crisis in the house. For example, if someone acted out because he was mad and he was getting all the staff's attention, I pretended I was mad at the staff because they were treating him unfairly.

I had a hard time forming healthy friendships, and I had a hard time fitting in with the other boys. I longed for recognition and attention. By getting involved in someone else's crisis, I not only got attention, but I also hoped my behavior would show the other kids that I was cool and that I was on their side. This worked at times but failed most of the time.

I could tell that my enjoying doing this frustrated the staff, but it was fun. Rich, the house manager, really reprimanded me about my behavior. He told me he felt I could succeed in this program. He said I needed to stop paying attention to the other boys and to just focus on myself, on my own goals. Of course when the other boys were around I laughed it off and acted like I didn't care what Rich had to say. But when Rich pulled me aside and we talked one on one, I listened. I respected what he had to say and knew that he was honest in what he was saying. Why I had such respect for him I really didn't know. There was just something about his way of doing things that put me at ease. Rich and I butted heads a lot of the time though. This was because I rebelled against what was probably his best asset, consistency.

Rich took me out one day alone to get some ice cream and confided to me that he was leaving Victor permanently in order to go back to school. I was deeply saddened at that moment. My heart sank. Rich was a man who was strict but fair. I could talk to him and feel safe. He was almost like a father to me.

Now he was leaving. This was a big blow to me and I was not sure how to handle it. After being unable to trust anyone for years and years, I'd started to put my trust into this one man. Now he was going away.

This was exactly what I was always afraid would happen. The people who I finally had drummed up the courage to tell my secrets to, to confide in, would abandon me like all the others. I felt betrayed and lost. Memories I'd long suppressed began to resurface, memories of abandonment, lies, and fear.

For a moment I was afraid I wouldn't know what to do without him. I told him that I really appreciated everything he had done for me and the time he had always taken to listen to me. I said he would be missed, at least by me. He assured me that I would be OK and that I must continue to put into practice what he had taught me. I agreed. We finished our ice cream and left. As we drove back to the house I was overwhelmed with emptiness. I was beginning to feel all alone again. I knew I was losing someone who would make sure I was on the right track. What was I going to do when he was no longer there? How would I know what to do or how to live when he was gone? How would I succeed? Would I lose my way again?

Rich left Victor a few weeks later. After he left I felt very lonely, yet I strove to keep the promise I'd made to him. I would work harder toward excelling and being mindful of what he had taught me. A few of the tools and suggestions he left me with included:

1. Realize that you have no control over what happened to you in the past.

2. Always remember that your future can be whatever you want it to be.

3. When you're angry, take a deep breath in through your nose and exhale through your mouth. This lets you regain self-control and lets you focus on what's going on.

4. Realize you are a good person and you have a lot going for you.

5. Don't keep anger inside. Always talk about what's on your mind so it doesn't build up and spiral out of control.

6. Patience. Good things will happen but they will take time. Make goals and stick to them.

After Rich left I turned my attention to another staff member, Jeff. He was also a cool, self-confident guy. He seemed to understand me. He talked to me and not at me. He never judged me and he always spoke in a calm tone of voice. He never put me down or called me names, and he respected me enough to tell me the truth. He was stern when he needed to be. He always made sure that he was consistent with rules and was always fair when giving me consequences for bad behavior.

Consistency is very important for kids with Reactive Attachment Disorder and he understood this. As a reward for my good behavior and doing well in the program, Jeff took me fishing. He loved to fish and so did I. It was perfect. We left the chaos of the group home when we went on these trips. That was important to me. I did not want to have to worry about the other kids when I was trying to relax and have a good time.

When there were times I was sad and did not know who to turn to, Jeff was there to help me. He would hug me and tell me everything would turn out just fine. He never hugged me in front of the other kids because he knew I would be made fun of. He respected that. He knew I had put up a wall and that I refused to let anyone see how I truly felt. Jeff was a good guy. He now seemed to be just the person I needed. With him I could start to let my guard down again.

For the first time in my life I felt that I was ready to start building my future. I had now learned that my life could be whatever I wanted it to be. I had control over that. I had started to mature over time in the group home. In part I had just grown up. But mostly, I had learned a lot. Now I started to see that other people (staff, Dad and Mom, Hale) really did care about me. I started to see that my actions, good or bad, elicited a reaction in kind, either good or bad. I realized that if I continued down the negative path I had followed, that I would get bad results. I was ready to start to open up and talk about my feelings. But it would be a slow, cautious process.

During my time at Victor I had my ups and downs. There was no fixed date that I would leave there. That depended on my behavior and progress. I ended up staying for two years. Near the end of my two-year stay I began to excel and do really well. I moved up in the levels and eventually reached level four. This was the level a child reached if he did really well and was almost ready to graduate from the program.

I was very proud of myself and how far I had come. I had seen very few other boys graduate and leave the program in the two years I had been at Victor. Mine was one of the success stories.

Being promoted to level four was a huge accomplishment for me. I even received a Resident of the Month award for it. Everyone was impressed with the progress I'd made since coming to Victor. I was now able to accept responsibility for things I did. I now knew a lot better what was right and what was wrong. I was now able to change my thought processes. I stopped running away. I stopped getting into trouble at school. I began to have more respect for people around me.

I'd become a very different person and more mature. I'd finally accepted the fact that I could do nothing about what had happened to me in my past. I finally began to believe that I had a future, and that my future could be whatever I wanted it to be. All I needed to do was to continue using the techniques I'd learned at Victor. These included setting goals that were attainable in a reasonable amount of time.

I began to see things differently. I was ready to face the future and whatever would come my way. For the first time in my life I was hopeful. I knew that I would have to continue working on my problems, but I was confident that the progress I'd made at Victor would benefit me in the future.

With Victor's help I'd been able to turn my life around. I'd worked hard on controlling my anger, on ignoring negative influences, on admitting my mistakes, on accepting punishment doled out to me. I'd learned to take risks and open up to the staff little by little about what I was feeling. I'd forced myself to change the way I thought about things. And I'd learned that telling the truth was better than lying.

I accepted the fact that my biological mother Leanne would never be coming to get me and that Jerry and Suzanne were now my mom and dad. They were my parents. I was ready to call them Mom and Dad. However, I still did not have a close bond with them because of all my acting out in prior years and then being away in a group home for two years.

Towards the end of my stay at Victor, the Executive Director informed me that because I was doing so well, I'd be eligible to graduate from the program and go home in about two months. I was excited but reserved. I'd spent two years at Victor and had developed bonds with certain people. I was unsure what life would be like on the outside.

I called my parents' house to let them know I would be graduating and to tell them I could not wait to come home. I spoke with my dad. Mom didn't seem to be around anywhere where I could talk to her. Dad said he was very proud of me for making such amazing progress. But then he told me point blank that I could not come home. He said he thought I only wanted to come home so I could live closer to my sister Jessica. He kept saying he didn't think I really wanted to be with him and Mom, that it didn't feel at all to him that I wanted them as my parents. He went on to say he hadn't seen any evidence of closeness, of attachment, at all. I pleaded with him and told him just how wrong he was. But he did not seem to believe me. I could not get him to listen. I asked to speak with my mom, but was told she was out of the country traveling.

This of course devastated me. For the first time I cared deeply about what my dad and mom thought of me. Here I was, more mature than I'd ever been, more respectful than ever before, and my dad could not see that. I'd learned to tell the truth no matter what and he thought I was lying. I was confused and hurt by that. I slammed down the phone and let out a big angry yell. Then I stomped out of the house office.

But that was as far as it got. I'd grown up and was finally able to control my anger. I sat with the staff afterwards and told them how I felt. I told them that I was very hurt and could not believe I could not go home. The whole time I was at Victor I thought that if I could just show a positive change, that Dad and Mom would be proud of me and take me back. This was a huge let down. Being able to express my feelings was very good for me, a big step for me, and one which again showed me how much progress I'd made.

And where was Mom? Why couldn't I talk to her? Why wasn't she reachable? She would believe me. She would listen to me. She would want me. She would see who I'd become. Where on earth was she? (I would later learn that she had been working as an air courier in Southeast Asia — Thailand, Malaysia, and Singapore. She was moving from place to place, had no phone, and was, for the most part, unreachable.)

So then the next question became: Where was I to go when I was released from the group home? My social worker Hale then told me I'd be able to go live with my sister Julia. Her family now lived in Moorpark, near Los Angeles. I was excited. I could not wait. I was now 15 years old and I was more than ready to start my new life. The drive from Redding to Moorpark in the agency van was an incredibly long one. Two staff members drove me there. During the long drive I kept wondering how things would work out at my sister's. As I was used to group home life and the way they did things, my new living situation was going to be different, but I was certain I was up to it.

We arrived at Julia's late in the evening. Julia's parents, Anne and Gary, were happy to see me. They each hugged and kissed me and thanked the staff for driving me down there. I turned to the staff, gave them each a big hug, and then started to cry. I was going to miss them a lot. I was also going to miss the stability I'd had for the past two years. They told me I could call Victor any time I needed help with the transition to my sister's house. I thanked them and assured them I would call. They got into the van and pulled out of the driveway. As I watched the van leave, I wondered what my future would be like. I just hoped I could truly hold on to and even continue building upon the success I'd achieved. I wiped the tears from my eyes and turned and walked into the house.

Part Four

Moving on — life in the real world

10 Moving out ... and on

This was a new beginning for me. By now I had completely turned my life around. It had taken a few years and a lot of work, but I felt confident I could handle anything that would come my way. I'd learned how to deal with my anger. I'd started to learn to let go of my past and realize that I had a future. What the future would hold was still to be determined but I realized that it was totally up to me. I had the power to do that. The future was in my own hands.

But for now I had to focus on the present and figure out how to adjust to normal life again. A few weeks after coming to stay at my sister's, I was informed by Anne, my sister's mother, that their family was going on a vacation to England to visit their relatives. They had planned the trip before they knew I'd be coming to stay with them and it was now too late to arrange to take me with them. So plans were made for me to go stay temporarily with Jessica, the sister I'd recently met who lived in Turlock, California. I was excited about having the chance to spend this time with her. It would hopefully let me get to know her better. I could not wait to go. My sister Julia drove me all the way to Turlock.

Turlock lies about 300 miles north of Los Angeles, in California's central valley. Jessica and her family lived in a small white farmhouse in the countryside. I liked the atmosphere as soon as we drove up. I was in my element. I was never one for big cities or even suburbs and I always had a love of the outdoors and country living. I met Jessica's stepmother and father Jane and Larry, who welcomed me with open arms. They seemed excited to see me and gave me lots of hugs. I appreciated the affection. I felt a little out of place though because of the way I was dressed. They were accustomed to cowboy boots and wrangler pants here. I wore oversized shirts with baggy pants that were falling off my hips, my style at the time.

I learned they owned their own construction business. I'd never seen big machines like a backhoe or dump truck up close. Both were parked in the backyard. I thought that was really neat. I found out that, like me, they loved to fish. That sat well with me. That was something I was passionate about. The whole atmosphere in their house was calm, friendly and warm. I felt really comfortable there. I stayed for the two weeks Julia and her family were in England. I was quite sad to leave their place.

Although I was looking forward to seeing my sister Julia again, part of me wanted to keep the life I was living here at Jessica's that I seemed so in tune with. At Jessica's I had a great time fishing, learning to shoot different guns, playing with the family dogs, and being part of what felt to me was a close-knit family. I did not want that to end, so I had reservations about going back to Moorpark.

Then I remembered what I'd been taught at Victor about how to deal with situations that made me feel uneasy or upset. I opened up and talked to my sister Julia on the drive back home and let her know how I felt about not wanting to leave Jessica's. She understood but encouraged me to give her family a chance. I loved Julia and agreed. But the chance I was willing to give them would last only a few weeks.

I was enrolled in Moorpark High School and was ready to start my sophomore year, grade 10, in just a few weeks. I already had concerns about attending that school. I remembered how my first year in high school had been when I was in the group home and I sure did not want to repeat that. I would now have to make friends all over again and I wasn't sure I was ready for that.

Julia's parents, Anne and Gary, were wonderful people, with kind and generous hearts, but their lifestyle was something I was not used to. They were Jewish and they practiced their religion openly. My sister Julia was used to that since she had been adopted by them at age seven. But I wasn't used to practicing any religion. Also, daily life around their house was calm, quiet, and monotonous — always the same. Nothing really excited me about anything in the daily routine. I was bored.

When Anne and Gary found me crying in my room, they tried hard to cheer me up. But nothing they said or did seemed to help. I started feeling old emotions coming back, ones of uncertainty and reticence. I felt that way any time I began to feel uncomfortable in any given situation. My anger started to come back too. My sister Julia and I got into arguments over even the smallest things. I was rarely able to pinpoint what I was angry about or who I was angry with. All I knew was, when I felt really out of place somewhere, out of my element, my really angry feelings resurfaced. I didn't know why this was happening and it really worried me.

One night I got so angry I grabbed a video my parents had made of me playing the trumpet and completely destroyed it. Everyone was upset with me and I started not to care again. I found where Gary kept his liquor and occasionally took a few drinks. I still smoked and that was a problem for Anne and Gary as well. They were loving caring people but I just couldn't bring myself to get close to them. When Anne came to talk to me alone, I often moved away from her and felt very ill at ease. I would get very tense and my breathing would start to get heavy. I found it very hard at age 15 to really feel like part of this family. I felt like an outsider who was just passing through on a long journey. What else was new?

One night I excused myself from the table and ran to my room sobbing. Anne came in and sat next to me. I think she knew what was going on. She sensed that I was unhappy in this environment. I sat there and talked to her about what I was feeling. I explained to her that I did not like it at her house. I told her that I felt lonely and that I didn't feel I belonged there. She tried to ask questions about why I felt that way, but I had no real answers to give her. I just told her that I'd felt more comfortable in Turlock at Jessica's. Julia's household was very quiet and laid back. It reminded me very much of my parents' place in Palo Alto. Turlock however was different. Jessica's house was in the country where there was always some fun activity going on. And I could smoke, fish, shoot guns and, in a way, do what I wanted.

Anne agreed to call my social worker Hale. After being sent to the group home, Hale once again had taken on my case as my social worker since he had known me most of my life. He again stepped into the role of the person making sure I was properly taken care of. He would resolve any issues involving my living situation. He was one of the most caring, attentive people I'd ever known. Anne wanted to talk to him about moving me to Turlock where I'd been happy.

In no way, shape, or form did I not love my sister Julia or her parents Anne and Gary. But I needed to feel at home. I needed to be able to relax, to let that defensive wall I'd built around me come down, and to be in my element. My social worker Hale told me that I could not go live with my sister Jessica and her family in the country. I don't remember why. But he said I could go stay with Jessica's step-dad and mom, Ron and Judy. This way at least I could live near my sister Jessica, as both families lived close to each other.

Judy was married to Jessica's dad Larry when Jessica was adopted when she was six months old. Years later they divorced and each remarried. Larry married Jane and Judy married Ron. I had met Ron and Judy when I'd gone to Turlock the first time and we seemed to hit it off.

I agreed to go live with Ron and Judy and a few days later I was driven to Turlock by Julia and her mother Anne. Ron was a well-known taxidermist who ran his business out of his home. I was fascinated by all the animal heads hanging on the walls and the animals he was currently working on in his garage. He even had a glass case in the living room with whole stuffed animals in it, real stuffed animals. He also had awards hanging on his wall from many people honoring him for his work.

Judy was a real estate agent specializing in country houses. She and Ron lived in a nice modern home in central Turlock, close to shopping and the high school. My first impression upon meeting them was that they were easy going and easy to get along with. They both seemed to be very warm-hearted people who loved kids very much. They were very happy to meet me and welcomed me into their family.

Things at Ron and Judy's would soon not work out either. I still wanted the lifestyle Jessica's other family had shown me in the country. There was just something about that way of living that I was attracted to, that drew me in, that captivated me. I also didn't like the fact that Ron and Judy wouldn't let me go see or even talk to my parents.

I wondered if I would ever be happy where I was living. I attended Turlock High School as a sophomore. My sister Jessica also went there, as a senior. It was cool to attend school with her. I had someone to look up to and she was there to help me get accustomed to the new school. She was popular in school and I was welcomed by all of her friends.

One day at school Jessica approached me and asked if I still wanted to come stay with her and her family out in the countryside. I didn't even think twice. I said, "Absolutely," then rode home with her the same day. I was not really worried about what Ron and Judy would think. I just knew that I'd gotten what I wanted and that was all that mattered.

11 First love

I now was 17 years old. I continued going to school at Turlock High School and also worked as a bag boy at a grocery store in town. This is where I met the girl I thought I would marry. She came in to shop one day and I saw her looking my way. I looked behind me to see what she was staring at but no one was there. I turned back around and continued to bag groceries for the customers.

At school the next day I saw the same girl walking down the hallway. As she walked by me her girlfriend pushed her into me. She laughed and then went straight to her class. Her friend was in my class. During class she handed me a note from the same girl. The note said she liked me and wanted to get to know me. I blushed and smiled and thought that was really neat. No girl had ever seemed to notice me before.

I found out from her girlfriend that her name was Nicole and that she was sixteen. She was a very pretty girl, with medium build, long blond hair and blue eyes. I'd always told myself that I would marry a girl with blond hair and blue eyes. The next day at work Nicole came in again and on my break we started to talk. She told me she lived with her grand-mother in the pink house just across the street from the store. Sure enough, there was a pink two story house directly across the street from the store. I thought that was really neat.

She called me later that night at my sister's house. We must have talked for at least an hour. We talked a lot about our common interests, like what music we liked and what foods we enjoyed most. I was so excited I had "butterflies" in my stomach. I was so happy that a girl was interested in me, especially such a pretty one. We decided we would go out on a date together the next day, then see what happened from there. We quickly became boyfriend and girlfriend. I thought I was one lucky guy to have a girlfriend like her. We hung out together and shot pool at the local billiards hall in Turlock. We partied at friends' houses on several occasions. I took her to the gym and we lifted weights together. Occasionally we went out to dinner together too.

Every free moment we had we either talked on the phone or saw each other. She came to my work and we ate lunch together during my breaks. Sometimes I sent flowers and balloons to her house. I felt it really was turning into a serious relationship. Things could not be going any better. She was the one I lost my virginity to at age 17. To me that sealed the deal. We were meant for each other. Even her family liked me.

Nicole made me feel happy. She was warm, energetic, and fun to be around. She loved to laugh and joke around. She was free-spirited and never let anything sway her mind. She loved to hang around me and was always there to cheer me up when I felt down or I was unsure about something. Every time I talked to her or hugged her, I felt like I was all that mattered to her. She liked me for the person I was and never tried to change anything about me.

However, once I turned eighteen, things started to change. Now I was legally an adult and she was still sixteen and legally a minor. It was illegal for an adult to have sex with a minor. Because of this, Jessica's stepmother Jane told me I could no longer see Nicole. Needless to say, that did not sit well with me and I was not going to listen. I loved this girl and no matter what anyone said, no one was going to change my mind. Tensions quickly arose in the house. So at age 18 I moved out on my own into an apartment in Turlock. Freedom at last! I could do what I wanted, make my own decisions, and do things on my own schedule.

When I finished high school I thought about going to college, but I wanted to take some time off first just to relax. I also really didn't know what I wanted to do with my life. I did know I wanted to experience living on my own though. I found a roommate, Jessica's boyfriend's brother. I'd saved some money while working at the grocery store so I agreed to pay the bills until my roommate got a job. Then he could pay me back. This never happened of course, so I told him to move out.

I soon realized that living on my own at such a young age was probably not a good idea. Yet, ironically, choosing to do this ultimately started me on a path that led to success. That path would be a long and difficult one however, one riddled with many obstacles along the way.

I no longer talked to my sister Jessica's parents Larry and Jane because they did not approve of my relationship with Nicole. They felt that I was rushing things and that I should not be dating someone under age 18 since it was against the law. As I was used to figuring out ways to make things work, I wasn't about to let people who disagreed with me get in my way.

I soon had another roommate, Nicole. Her living situation at her grandmother's was not working out. Her grandmother, who was her legal guardian, was ill and could no longer take care of her. So Nicole needed a place to stay. I had a close friend in high school whose family was like a second family to me. I spoke with his parents and they agreed Nicole could come live with them.

But after a few weeks living there Nicole came to live with me in my apartment. She was still in high school, but it was now summer and school was out. I knew we would have time to figure out how she was going to get to school in the fall. (I didn't drive because I was still having epileptic seizures. As such, the State of California wouldn't let me get a driver's license.) I was excited that Nicole wanted to come live with me. I would finally get to spend uninterrupted intimate time with her. We had been together for three months. It was about time.

But, as I would soon to find out, that would come at a price. She told me one night that her stomach was hurting and she did not know why. After we tried everything we could think of to get rid of the pain, we finally called a taxi and went to the hospital. It was there that they told us Nicole was two months pregnant. She had turned seventeen but was still a minor. I was eighteen.

My initial reaction to hearing the news was that I thought for sure I'd be going to jail. I was scared to death to face her family, but I knew I had to. She was crying because she didn't know what to do. I held her hand, told her not to worry, and that I'd do everything I could to make sure she and this baby were cared for and provided for. Even though I didn't have a college education, I promised her that I'd work two or three jobs if necessary in order to give her and the baby everything they needed. I would not let my girlfriend and soon to be son or daughter be subjected to neglect like I had been so many years before.

Nicole's aunt was in the hospital room with us when we found out that Nicole was pregnant. I'd called her to let her know that Nicole was in the hospital and she met us there. When she heard about the pregnancy she did not yell or seem upset with me. She turned to me and assured me that everything would be fine.

Nicole's uncle, however, was fit to be tied. He couldn't even look me in the eye. I thought for sure he was going to yell at me. I was also sure he was going to have me arrested for having sex with an underage girl, for statutory rape. Both Nicole's aunt and uncle seemed to know I was not a bad guy however. Nicole's family never filed any charges against me. I was relieved, to say the least. I knew I was not a deadbeat and so did Nicole. We both knew that I'd do everything I could to make sure Nicole and the baby were taken care of. I had no college education, few marketable skills, and was working at a minimum wage job. I was unsure exactly how I was going to support the two of them, but I was determined I would.

The next few months were rough. The grocery store cut back my hours from 40 to 18, so I desperately needed additional income. I started a second job at a wireless phone company some thirty miles away. That job paid $8.00 an hour, which was a lot more than I was making at the store. I still did not have a car or even a driver's license, so I carpooled with my next door neighbor who also worked at the wireless company. Things were starting to look up. I was excited about the baby coming and about having my own family. But I had no idea how hard being a young father would turn out to be. I also did not realize at the time that, with only a high school education, supporting a family would prove to be a very difficult struggle.

Then we got the news that Nicole's father was being released from jail, where he'd been serving time for using drugs. He had nowhere to go so I offered to let him come stay with us. I was the type of person who would give the shirt off his back to help someone. Nicole was happy and thanked me. I knew from past talks with her about her father that he had used drugs and that he had spent time in jail as a result. But I believed people could change, as I had, so I had no problem giving him a chance. I believed that everyone deserved a second chance. He was also the father of my soon-to-be wife and the grandfather of my soon-to-be child.

Nicole was not aware of the fact that I was going to ask her to marry me in the near future. I just wanted to make sure that we were not going to get married just because of having a baby. I wanted us to be married for more than that. I wanted us to marry because we were in love and we wanted to spend the rest of our lives together, with or without kids. Because we were still so young and our lives were just taking shape, I wanted to be sure that we would want to stay together through thick and thin. I wanted our child to have a healthy, two parent household filled with happiness and joy.

About three months later it still seemed clear that we had a future together, a lifelong committed future. I bought Nicole a small but sweet diamond engagement ring. I gave it to her and told her I was going to marry her. That was it. It was not really a proposal, just a statement of fact on my part. I really loved her. I had "butterflies." I smiled all the time. There was just something between us.

I had no idea my decision to let her father stay with us, and my trusting that he'd kicked his drug habit, would turn out to be one of the worst decisions I could have made. I had no idea then that this one bad decision would lead me down a dark road, a road that led to a place of utter confusion, to despair, to hopelessness. I had no idea then that the hopelessness I would come to feel would result in me almost ending my life.

Part Five

Real love — fatherhood

12 Instant love

Our son Daniel was born in February 1999, weighing 8 pounds 3 ounces. I was in the delivery room to help welcome him into the world. I cried with joy so much that day. He was the most beautiful boy I'd ever seen. I instantly had a love for him. I remember holding him for the first time. When he opened his eyes, tears filled mine. I could not believe that I'd helped make this precious little human being. I looked at him and thought about how much I'd grown up, about how I'd beaten all the odds — all that, and how I was now able to be a father to someone so special.

I called Dad and Mom. They were very happy to hear about the baby. They were against unmarried couples having children however, so they urged us to get married right away.

Nicole's father seemed to bond well with Daniel. He even came up with our son's name — Daniel Glenn Hogsett. Glenn was her dad's name and Daniel was the name of a friend of his. I thought the name was perfect.

I'd just turned 19 the week before Daniel was born. Even though I very much wanted to be, I was by far not the perfect dad. The strain of now having a baby to take care of started to take a toll on my relationship with Nicole. We argued a lot and said things to each other that were downright hurtful. We fought mostly about her saying I didn't give her enough affection, that I didn't hold her hand as we walked, that I didn't hug or kiss her enough, and that I didn't show her enough attention. I thought I did the best I could, but I just didn't know how. I was afraid of closeness and afraid of intimacy, because closeness in the past just resulted in painful losses. Ironically my inability to be emotionally available to Nicole, my inability to attach to her, resulted in me losing her. My history repeated itself. We grew distant from each other and our relationship started to go downhill about two months after Daniel was born.

At night when Daniel cried I always told Nicole to get up to see what he needed. I was the only one working and I had to get up early to go to work. So why should I get up at night? That was my way of thinking. This of course put an even bigger strain on our relationship. On some nights I went out with my friends and even invited them over to our apartment when I knew I should be spending time with Nicole instead. I was young, far from perfect, and I still had a lot of growing up to do.

Soon I was completely stressed out. I did not know what to do or who to turn to. Everything I'd learned over the years about dealing with feeling angry seemed to vanish. The anger came back, big time. One night during an argument Nicole said she hoped I'd have an epileptic seizure in my sleep and die. That really hurt me, as seizures were a big problem in my life. I struggled with seizures growing up. I never knew when they would happen. I never knew if I'd be alone when I'd have a seizure or if I'd be with someone who knew what to do. This was serious to me and I wasn't going to let anyone, no matter who it was, say such hurtful things to me.

When Nicole said that to me I was so furious that I punched our bedroom door, making a hole in it. She then yelled at me for damaging the door. Then she made another comment that really pushed me over the brink. She told me that Daniel was not my child.

I lost it right then and there. I reacted in an instant, without thinking. Rage took over. I slapped Nicole across the face with my hand three times. Nothing around me at that point seemed real. I was consumed with anger and overcome with pent up frustration. I was also physically exhausted. Nicole covered her face with her hands and ran from the living room into the bedroom. I followed her and began screaming at her, telling her not to look at me. I knocked over some furniture and proceeded to punch a hole in the bedroom wall. She was terrified. At that point I felt I finally had control over her. Even her Dad tried to step in, but I told him to mind his own business. He told me that I'd better stop or else. I looked at him with piercing eyes and slammed the bedroom door right in his face. I did not care if he was older than I was. I did not care if he was Nicole's father. I did not care if he intimidated me. He needed to keep his face out of my business.

Just then another feeling came over me. Sadness. My chest started to hurt and my eyes started to water. I stepped back from the bed. Nicole was on the other side of the bed sitting on the floor with her face in her hands, crying. What was I doing? I did not know who I was anymore. This was not me. It couldn't be. I turned around and left the room, avoiding looking at Nicole's father, who was now sitting on the couch. I left the apartment and went for a long walk. I'd learned at Victor to go for a long walk in order to calm down. But I still needed to learn which things triggered my anger in order to prevent myself from getting that upset in the first place. I thought I wouldn't blame Nicole at all if she were gone when I returned.

But she was still there. Things calmed down a short while later and I told her how very sorry I was for what I'd done to her. But the damage had already been done and I could not undo it. I'd done something I thought I would never do. I'd slapped a woman. I felt like I was the lowest form of life, the worst possible being. I was so ashamed of the person I'd apparently become. I was not sure how I had let my anger progress to that point. But one thing was evident. I still had a really serious anger problem that needed to be addressed. And it needed to be addressed now.

Luckily for me the police were never called. Later I would discover something hidden in my apartment that would give me a clue why. I knew that Nicole's father had struggled with drug use, mainly marijuana and heroin. Before he came to stay with us he'd told me he no longer did drugs and that he was attending Alanon and Alcoholics Anonymous meetings. But I started to notice a change in him about a month into his stay with us. He would be gone for hours. Then he'd bring home all kinds of junk he'd found at yard sales or just sitting by the side of the road. He'd collect boxes of chains, bike parts, radio parts, you name it. I thought that this habit was really strange. He tinkered with things. One evening he brought home a radio, which he took apart and then put back together again. There was other very strange behavior too.

One night when Nicole, Daniel and I were at a friend's house across the street, I headed back to the apartment to grab a diaper for Daniel. Glenn was in the apartment. I knocked on the front door because it was locked. A woman wrapped in a towel opened the door. I asked her who she was. She gave me a dirty look and wanted to know who I was. When I told her I was the one who paid the rent in the apartment she opened the door for me. Then she went to Glenn's room. I was furious.

My apartment was not a place for women like that to come and go. My apartment was not intended to house people I did not know. I did not need these surprises. I confronted Glenn and told him in a stern voice that I did not approve of this situation and that the woman needed to go now. He apologized and she left. I was irritated. Something needed to be done.

I decided that one day while Glenn was at work I would do some snooping. Nicole and I were getting along again and she agreed to help me. What we found in a closet really angered me. It was a small brown leather pouch. When I opened it I found two syringes, a small piece of thin rubber hose, and a spoon with drug residue still on it. I knew right away what these things were. Glenn was still doing drugs, and he was doing them in the apartment where my son lived.

That was the final straw. We decided not to confront him at the time and to just wait until he left to go to Oregon on vacation. He had a girlfriend who lived in Oregon and in a few days he was going to go visit her. As soon as he left on vacation, Nicole and I collected all of the junk in his room and took it to the dumpster. We then cleaned out his room, scrubbed it down, and redecorated it for our son. It became his nursery.

A short time later Glenn returned from Oregon with his girlfriend. When he saw all of his stuff was gone he was fit to be tied. To top it off, Nicole denied she ever took part in it. I was on my own. Now Nicole was on his side and I was left to take all the blame. I felt tricked. I also felt trapped. That night Nicole and I stayed up late talking. I asked her why she denied helping me clear out her father's things. She claimed it was because she was afraid her Dad might get upset with her. I thought, "Who cares if he gets upset? Look what he was doing in the apartment." But I left it at that.

Then she told me she was driving to Oregon with her dad and his girlfriend on a two-week vacation and that she was going to take Daniel. She thought we needed some time apart and I agreed. The next morning her bags were packed and Daniel was strapped in his car seat in her Dad's girlfriend's truck. I hugged Nicole and gave Daniel a kiss. She gave me the phone number of her Dad's girlfriend's house where she'd be staying and said to call her in a few days because she'd be on the road driving. I said OK and watched them drive off. But, as they drove off, I couldn't help but wonder why Nicole had taken all of Daniel's clothes and everything else he had. I just looked forward to the time when they'd be back.

13 Instant loss

I had no idea then how much that day's events would change my life. Three days went by without hearing anything from Nicole. I was a little worried but I thought maybe they were not near a phone. I did not want to bother her on her vacation. I tried to call her a few times and I left messages, but I still didn't hear from her. I just assumed they were busy and that Nicole would call when she had the chance.

I went to work as usual. I'd quit the grocery store job soon after they'd cut my hours way back. Then I'd been fired by the phone company for talking back to a rude customer. I guess I'd let the battles in my home life get to me at work. I now worked for a security company, Delta Force Security, in Turlock. I worked nights, seven nights a week, by my own choosing. Working hard was something that just came naturally to me. I was someone who couldn't sit still. I had to work.

After four days of not hearing from Nicole I began to worry. I called the phone number again she had given me. No one answered and I left another message. I'd already left quite a few. I missed her and Daniel a lot by now. I began to feel empty inside. Empty. Depressed. Lonely. I hadn't felt that empty since I'd been taken to the children's shelter by my biological mother Leanne when I was five years old. I stopped sleeping in our usual bed. Instead, I slept on the living room floor right next to the phone, hoping it just might ring and that I'd hear Nicole's voice on the other end.

She finally called a few days later. It had been about a week since she'd left. I was so happy to hear from her. She said she was doing fine but that I needed to stop calling her and harassing her. I was shocked. What was she talking about? I tried to get an answer from her. She apparently was upset with me. I thought I knew why. I had the feeling she was still upset because I'd slapped her that one awful day. Looking back now, I think Nicole had probably given up on our relationship after that fight and was planning to leave me all along. Since she must have felt so unsafe with me, she was probably just looking for a quick way out. I understood that and did not blame her at all. But I still loved and cared for her and my son and wanted to know how they both were doing.

Then she told me that she and Daniel weren't coming back at all and that she would be staying in Oregon with her Dad. She insisted that I stop calling her. Then she hung up the phone. It felt like my heart had just been ripped right out of my chest and stomped on. I cried so much that day that after a while it felt like there were no more tears left. I threw some of the furniture around the apartment. I hit the walls. I felt completely helpless. I felt cheated. I'd been betrayed, big time. I flew into a rage!

I ran from my apartment for about two miles to Nicole's grand-mother's house to tell her about the phone call I'd just received. She called Nicole and confirmed what I'd just heard. Her grandmother apologized to me but also said that Nicole was making her own choices and that there was nothing she could do about it. I was fairly sure that Nicole had talked to her grandmother about our problems, because she and her grandmother were very close.

I then ran another two miles across town to my best friend Dwayne's house. I did not want to be alone. I needed someone to talk to and to be with, someone I could trust and who could understand how I felt. When I arrived there I was in tears. Dwayne's Mom let me in. I told her what had happened and she said I could stay at her place as long as I needed to. My boss said he understood my situation and told me to take as much time off as I needed.

Dwayne's Mom gave me a muscle relaxant to calm my nerves and soon I was so tired from crying and from running that I fell asleep. When I awoke I was numb physically and emotionally. I thought for a moment that it had all been just a nightmare. But when I saw where I was I knew it was real. I felt nothing other than total hopelessness. All I could think of was my son. I really loved him. I loved him more than I'd ever loved anyone. I even loved him more than my sister. And now he had been taken from me, stolen. I had no idea when, or even if, I would ever see him again.

I kept thinking about all the what ifs. What if I hadn't slapped Nicole? What if I'd shown her more affection and love? What if I had gotten up at night with Daniel like I should have? Would I still be in this predicament? Would my son and the woman I'd loved so much still be in my life? Things were looking really grim.

At that moment I just lost my will to live. Daniel and Nicole were everything to me and I'd now lost them both. I was overwhelmed by helplessness and depression. That night, while I was still staying at Dwayne's, suddenly and without much thought, I grabbed my bottle of Tegretol, the medication I'd been taking to control my epileptic seizures. I knew that if I swallowed enough pills I could die. It was the only way I knew to make all the pain go away.

I poured about 15 or 20 pills into my hand. I looked at them for an instant, glanced around to make sure no one was watching, then swallowed them quickly with a glass of milk that I'd taken from the refrigerator. I wanted the quick way out. I wanted not to have to live this very painful life anymore. I sat there for a minute, not really thinking about what I'd just done. I wondered how long it would take for the pills to take effect. I wanted to end my life. I no longer felt I had anything to live for.

The next thing I remember is Dwayne's sister coming into the room and seeing the open bottle of pills next to me. She asked me what was going on and what I had done. I said nothing. She went to her mother and said something to her. I got up and left the house. I started to walk down the street but Dwayne came and stopped me. He asked me if I had taken the pills. I told him no. But by then things had started to happen. I began to feel a little dizzy. My heart started to beat faster and faster. I was stumbling all over the road. Dwayne grabbed my arm, walked me back to his house, sat me down in the garage, then called the paramedics. At that point I could not see clearly and was not sure what was happening.

I remember the police holding my arms down because they were flailing all over the place. Then I remember waking up in an ambulance, strapped down and unable to move. I was crying, but I had no idea why. The paramedics told me I was going to be fine. I was taken to a hospital bed in the emergency room, where they asked me some questions. That was the last thing I remembered.

I awoke the next day in a regular hospital room. I had a funny feeling in my throat. The nurse explained that they'd fed a tube through my nose down into my stomach to pump out all the medication I'd ingested. They'd also pumped in activated charcoal in liquid form to help alleviate the effects of the overdose. These tubes had slightly irritated my throat. I also noticed that a catheter had been inserted into my penis to help drain my bladder. I was strapped to the bed because I was still having seizures due to the overdose. Tegretol controlled my seizures, but oddly, one of the side effects of an overdose was also seizures. I had a massive headache and I was really confused. I'd survived, but in a way, I wished I hadn't.

A mental health worker came to talk to me in the hospital. He told me that ending my life was never the answer and that I was going to be taken to a facility to help me get through the feeling of wanting to give up hope. I had no choice about going there because I'd now been medically assessed to be a danger to myself. Because of this I was placed on a three-day hold. California law allowed patients to be placed on a three-day hold if they posed a danger to themselves or others. The patient couldn't leave the facility unless he or she was released by a psychiatrist. An ambulance came and took me to a mental health facility, Stanislaus Behavioral Health Center in Modesto.

I was now 19 years old and had completely given up on life, this time for good. To me life was now useless and utterly meaningless. Everyone I'd ever loved had been ripped from me, torn away. I was here on earth physically, but emotionally I had checked out. Everything around me was fuzzy and nothing made sense. I felt like I was trapped in a never-ending nightmare, one that kept getting worse and worse.

My stay at the mental health facility was difficult. I was only supposed to be there for three days. However, the therapists who talked to me still thought I posed a risk. They thought I could possibly try to kill myself again if I were let out too soon. So I was held for another fourteen days. I understood why they needed to hold me longer, but part of me just wanted to get out of there in order to complete what I'd started to do at Dwayne's.

At the Behavioral Health Center I attended daily group therapy sessions. Hearing similar stories from other people in the group helped a little. I learned that I could make it through this difficult time. I saw that I was not alone and that other people understood me. But that did not take away the emptiness I was still feeling inside. No words or assurance put me at ease. I was still missing my son terribly. I longed for him almost every waking moment. I just could not heal without him.

One day I took a pencil and frantically started to rub the eraser on the back of my hand in several places, causing burns. As a result I was placed in a room and strapped down to a bed until I was calm. The next day I took a piece of hard plastic and broke it until it had a sharp edge. I stood in my room and began to cut my wrists in several places with it. Blood spewed everywhere, spattering the walls, the floors, and the bed. I did this because I was so angry and it still felt like doing this gave my anger a natural release. I so desperately wanted to feel something again, hurt, sadness, whatever. Anything but anger. I just wanted to feel something. Anything. By cutting myself I was able to still feel human. I was able to see the blood as anger, anger that was rushing out of my body.

The staff came immediately and held my arms so I couldn't continue to hurt myself. Then the medical doctor came, determined the cuts were not deep enough to need stitches, and cleaned me up. The psychiatrist came and gave me a shot of Adivan to calm me down. I was put into a padded room and strapped to a bed until I was calm. I was then transferred to a unit for high risk patients.

Days went by and I was making good progress. At the end of my seventeen-day stay the doctors felt I was ready to be released to an assisted short term living facility to see how I'd do. There I'd continue to get therapy, but I'd be allowed to come and go freely.

I was at the new place for three days when a patient I'd met at the Behavioral Health Center offered to let me come stay with her. I accepted. Her name was Suzette and she lived in Sonora, California, a town in the Sierra foothills near Sacramento. I thought it would be good to be around someone like her who understood what I was going through. She promised me that I could talk to her about anything at any time. She wanted to help me.

Staying in Sonora was a short-lived experience, because once you do something, then it just becomes easier the next time around to do it again. This was very true in my case. In Sonora I was lonely again. The more I was alone, the more I became obsessed with thinking about my son and what Nicole had done to me. And that was not a good thing. Suzette always seemed to be working, so I could not talk to her when I needed to. There was really nothing there for me to do. The less my day was filled with productive things, the more I thought about Daniel.

One night I began to lose hope again. Everything I saw and every song I heard on the radio reminded me of him. I reached for my bottle of pills again. This time I ingested more than I had the first time. I just wanted all the pain to go away. This was the only way I knew how to make that happen, and to make that happen right away.

I sat in a chair, waiting for the medication to take effect. A short while later there was a knock at the door. It was a Sonora police officer. He said Suzette had tried to call to check on me from work but she couldn't reach me. She got worried and called the police to come check on me. When they arrived they noticed that I was acting a little strange. Again I felt dizzy and my speech began to slur. The officer told me to get into his car so he could take me to the local hospital to get checked out.

When we arrived all I remember is throwing up all over the place. I awoke there three days later and found out I'd been in a coma for three days. The hospital staff told me that if the police hadn't come when they did, that I would have died. During the days I was in the coma they weren't so sure I'd survive. They said it was touch and go. I spent another week in the hospital, then was driven back to the mental health facility in Modesto. I was again placed on a three-day hold because they determined that I still posed a danger to myself. But this time I stayed only three days. I was prescribed Zoloft to help me deal with my depression.

I was then told I'd been accepted into a program that had just started in Modesto to help kids between the ages of 18 and 21 who had mental health issues. The program was called Families First Visions. It was a unique concept. They would house us in apartments, usually with a roommate who was also in the program. They would assist us with our education by helping us apply to college. They'd also help us find jobs, learn new skills, and attend support meetings. They offered a wide range of activities aimed at getting us back on our feet.

I was placed in an apartment in Turlock located right behind the apartment where I'd lived with Nicole and my son. For some reason that did not bother me much. I could see the upstairs window of my old apartment. On some occasions I stared at that window and wondered again about the what ifs.

I was finally coming to terms with what had happened. I knew that I should not have slapped Nicole. I knew that I could have been a better father and provider. I felt guilty that I hadn't been the man I should have been. I felt guilty that I'd put so much responsibility on Nicole's shoulders. I felt guilty that I did not treat her the way she should have been treated. I started to understand why she had left and I no longer blamed her. I knew I wouldn't want to stay around and suffer abuse if I were in her shoes.

I saw the Families First Visions program as a real opportunity, a real second chance at life, the real break I needed. My rent would be paid and grocery money would be given to my roommate and me every month. Our utilities would be paid too. All the financial burdens would be taken care of. With those stresses out of the way, I could now focus on making something of my life.

I went back to work at Delta Force Security. They were happy to have me back and I was even promoted to supervisor. I really enjoyed that job. It did not pay much but it did not matter. Since all my bills were paid, my pay was pretty much just extra money I could save or use to buy what I wanted. My roommate did not work but he helped out around the apartment to keep it clean.

He was also nineteen and we got along well. I attended weekly group therapy sessions and even shared some of my life story with the other teens in the program. I still worked seven nights a week in order to keep busy and to keep my mind off the past. But I still couldn't get a driver's license because California required me to be seizure free for quite some time before I was allowed to drive. Since I'd been diagnosed as an epileptic and continued to have frequent seizures, I had little chance of getting a license.

I was lucky to have a really nice boss. He picked me up and drove me where I needed to be for work. Then he made sure someone picked me up in the morning at the end of my shift. Soon the apartment complex where I lived became an account for the security company. I was assigned to work there at night, patrolling the grounds and keeping things safe by making sure no one was breaking into cars or starting fights. Families First was always impressed with how well I was doing and they constantly praised me for working and accomplishing things. They were always just a phone call away if I needed anything, no matter what time of day or night it was.

My roommate and I were doing so well that we became the "poster children" for the Families First Visions program. It was hard to believe that just a short while ago I'd been so ready to die and that I'd tried twice. Now I was finally coming out of that depression. Now I felt like I had a purpose in life. I just did not know exactly what that purpose was yet. I knew that everything happened for a reason. I'd just not figured out yet what that reason was. I felt sure I would find that out in the near future. I felt confident that some day everything would be clear to me and that I'd come to learn why I'd gone through everything I had. I felt that if my life was starting to turn around for the better, then I was sure more good things lay ahead.

Part Six

Lifelong bonds — attachment

14 Brenda

In March 2000, at age 20, while I was in the security company office talking with my supervisors, two women walked in. One was Asian and had long flowing dark hair. The other was a tall blue eyed blonde. She had to have been at least 5 feet 10 inches tall. I walked out of the back room and pretended I was getting some paperwork so I could go see what they needed. I turned the corner and faced the front door where they were standing. My eyes lit up. I had a smile on my face. Boy, were they really good looking. And boy, did they smell good! I found out the blonde was filling out an employment application. I talked to her for a minute and told her I'd get the owner to help her with the application process. Then I turned around and started to walk back to the owner's office. I was blushing the whole time. I was instantly attracted to her. I wanted to get to know her. I wanted to get to know her right then and there.

I knew there was a special event coming up in a few days that our company was going to provide security for. I then found out that the woman who had come in and applied for a job had been hired. I asked my boss if she could be assigned to me for that special event day so I could train her. Since I was a supervisor he had no problem with that. I thought she was a real knockout and that this would be a great way to get to know her better.

The day of the special event I was working a double shift. It started at three in the afternoon and finished at eight the next morning. I saw the blonde woman out of the corner of my eye. She was all dressed up in her black security outfit and she looked great. I went over to her and introduced myself. She said her name was Brenda and that she remembered me from the office a few days before.

We worked closely together during her eight-hour shift that night. I explained how the company worked, the type of work we did, and so on.

She told me she knew the owners and that they had given her a card and told her to come down if she ever needed a job.

Before her shift was over at midnight, I asked her if she'd like to go to breakfast with me in the morning. She agreed and we decided to meet at 8 a.m. when my shift was over. However, as I still did not have a car or even a driver's license, I was a little embarrassed. I had to ask her if she could pick me up in the morning so we could go to breakfast. She smiled and said yes. I let out a big sigh. It was quite embarrassing to ask a girl out, then have to tell her that I didn't have a car to pick her up in. We exchanged phone numbers, then she left for the evening. I finished the rest of my shift, thinking about our upcoming breakfast date. For once it seemed things were looking up and going in the right direction.

Brenda and I soon spent every waking moment with each other. She lived in Modesto and I lived in Turlock, 14 miles away. Since I had an apartment, she came to stay with me on a regular basis. We loved to be around each other. We went on dates to movies, to play pool, to dinner. Whatever she wanted to do, we did. I even went to a clothing store and picked out an outfit I thought she might like. When she saw it that evening she laughed and said thank you, but that it was not her style. Oh well, I thought, at least I tried.

She laughed and smiled all the time. She smothered me with affection and gave me constant unending attention. She gave me a safe, loving refuge from the often harsh world around me. I felt safe and protected and at home. She wrapped me up in her arms. She massaged away my aches. Her constant touches seemed to heal me, to make my past go away, to make the horror of it all just fade away. Her presence alone was enough to start making me smile again. I was determined not to make the same mistakes with her that I'd made with Nicole. At age 20, for the first time in my life, I was able to start attaching to someone.

About a month later, in April 2000, I received an unexpected phone call. It was Nicole. The woman who had ripped my heart out, the woman who had made me want to die, the woman who had taken my son from me, had the nerve to call me! But, at the same time, I still desperately wanted to see my son. The phone number she had given me before she'd left had been changed, so I'd had no way of reaching her to know how my son was doing. Talking to Nicole could possibly be a way for me to get to know where my son was and to find out if I could visit him.

Nicole was kind and soft spoken on the phone. She wanted to know how I was doing and she apologized for what she had done. She said she was now living on her own and that she finally realized how hard it was to take care of an infant all by herself. I agreed with the things she was saying and continued to listen. She said Daniel was getting big and that he was doing well. She added that she and her dad didn't talk much any more and that she was doing the best she could as a single mother.

But I'd already moved on. I had already developed strong feelings for Brenda and we were very close. Nicole had left over a year earlier. Once I had met Brenda I had stopped loving Nicole. I had stopped needing her, stopped wanting her, and stopped obsessing about her. I was in no way, shape, or form willing to give up my relationship with Brenda just to risk being put through another potential heartache by Nicole. Nicole proceeded to tell me that she missed me and that she wanted another chance. Then I started thinking. I did not want to have any intimate romantic relationship with her. I had no intention of giving her a second chance. But I also knew how much I wanted to see my son.

As wrong as it might have been, I told her I'd give her another chance. The next thing I knew I was boarding a bus to travel to Oregon to see Nicole and Daniel. They lived in the coastal town of Gold Beach. I gave Nicole the impression that we were going to try to get back together. This I knew was a lie. The only thing that mattered to me as far as Nicole was concerned was for me to be able to see my son. I was willing to say or do anything for that chance. I had no intention whatsoever of getting back together with his mother.

The opportunity to see Daniel presented itself and I took full advantage of it. Brenda had flown to New Jersey in April for a family function. It was during this time that I bused to Oregon to see my son. I did not tell Brenda because I did not want her to have doubts about my loyalty to her. I also did not want to risk her calling Nicole and creating any problem that could possibly prevent me from seeing Daniel. I only planned to be in Oregon with Nicole for a few days. Then I'd return home before Brenda got home. Once I got home I'd tell Brenda in person.

I let my roommate in on the plan in case anyone tried to contact me. I also left specific instructions for him to tell Brenda a story I'd made up if she called. I phoned Nicole and gave her my bus number and arrival time so she'd be at the bus station in Gold Beach to get me. I boarded the bus and settled in for the seventeen-hour-long bus ride. The whole way there all I had on my mind was my son. When Nicole took him he was just four months old. Now he was a year-and-a-half. I wondered what he looked like now. I wondered how big he was. I wondered how much he was talking and walking. All these thoughts raced through my head. I did not sleep at all on the bus that night.

As the bus pulled into the bus station in Gold Beach the next afternoon, I saw Nicole immediately. She was the only one there waiting for the bus. She had a stroller with her. I hopped off the bus, grabbed my stuff, and went over to see her and my son. I gave her a hug and told her that it was nice to see her.

Then I looked down. There he was. He was huge! He was sleeping. He seemed peaceful and content. I wanted so much to pick him up and hold him but decided against it because I didn't want to wake him up. I just stood there for a few moments looking at him as tears ran down my cheeks. That moment was surreal. For that one moment nothing else mattered. For that one moment I was filled with love and joy. That was something I hadn't felt that deeply in a very long time. Sure, I now had strong feelings for Brenda, but my feelings as a father for my child were completely different. I did not want that day to end.

On the walk from the bus station to Nicole's apartment Daniel woke up and I took him out of the stroller. I gave him a big hug and held his hand as we walked the rest of the way. I was a Dad again. There was no other feeling like it in the world. I loved it. That night Daniel and I played with all his toys. We rolled around on the floor, laughed, and played some more. It was a dream come true for me.

Nicole and I talked after Daniel went to bed that night. We discussed all the past incidents and we both apologized for our behavior. I was ready to let go of the past and move on with the future. But for me that future did not include her. She wanted another chance for our relationship to work. That, I knew, was not going to happen. I was already in a happy, steady committed relationship with Brenda. As far as I was concerned, nothing was going to change that.

Despite being told about Brenda before I'd agreed to come, Nicole clearly wanted to just pick things up where we'd left off. For her it was as if Brenda weren't in the picture. She snuggled close to me, expecting a kiss. She touched me here, touched me there, hoping for something in return, hoping for closeness, hoping for a sign that all was well between us, looking for any sign I'd be a player in a future together with her. But I could offer nothing. I could not respond.

One night at Nicole's I got a phone call. It was Brenda. My roommate must have given her Nicole's phone number even though I'd clearly told him not to give it out. Brenda wanted to know what was going on. Nicole was in the other room, so I had to whisper. All I needed was for Nicole to hear me talking to Brenda. That, I knew, would cause an argument. I explained to Brenda that I was only at Nicole's to see my son and that I was coming right back. I told her I loved her and that I'd see her soon. Brenda did not fully understand what I was doing and for a minute she thought I was going to stay in Oregon. I promised her that I was coming back, that I'd moved on from Nicole, and that I was not going to stay in Oregon with a woman I was no longer in love with.

Just then Nicole started yelling, wanting to know who I was talking to and what the conversation was about. I explained to her that I'd come to Gold Beach to see my son and that was all. I said I'd told her what she wanted to hear because I felt that if I didn't, I'd lose the opportunity to see Daniel.

She became extremely irate and told me to pick either Daniel or Brenda. To me that seemed unfair. I told her I wouldn't pick one over the other, because, as far as I was concerned, there was no future for the two of us as a couple. I told her she was selfish for asking me to choose and that she needed to move on. She then went to stand in front of the doorway, blocking it so I couldn't leave to go for a walk to calm down. In the past I would have moved her from the doorway myself, but I was now able to control my anger by using the breathing techniques I'd learned at Victor. I asked her again in a calm tone of voice to please move, but again she refused.

Finally she told me that if I wanted to leave I had to sign a statement she had already written. It said I would give up all rights to Daniel if I left. Calling the police never crossed my mind. I knew the only way I was going to be allowed to leave was to sign that paper. I also thought that a handwritten copy would never hold up in court, if it came to that. So I signed it and walked out the door, suitcase in hand.

I walked to a local motel where I paid for a room and waited for the next bus in the morning to take me back to Modesto. I was sad to feel that I had to leave my son, but I was thankful I'd been able to see him. I knew that some day, somehow, some way, I was going to see him again. I was not going to let Nicole dictate where, if, and when that could happen. And I sure wasn't going to stay where I was not happy.

Brenda already knew what had happened because I'd called her from the motel. Because I'd used some of my money to pay for the room, I no longer had enough money to buy a bus ticket all the way to Modesto. But I lucked out. Brenda wired me the money I needed right away so I could pay for the entire trip. That was devotion, her willingness to help me out when I needed help so badly, in spite of what I'd done behind her back.

The next morning when the bus came I boarded and looked forward to going home. When we pulled into the Modesto bus station I was really glad to be back home. Now at least I had more fond memories of my son to hold on to. All I had though were memories because the photos that were taken in Oregon were taken on Nicole's camera. I was sure I wasn't going to see those photos anytime soon. I was beginning to feel that I was starting to get a handle on my frustrations and anger. I had managed to keep my calm throughout the whole ordeal, and that felt good.

Brenda grilled me about my whole trip and wondered why I hadn't told her. She was upset that I hadn't trusted her enough to talk to her about it. I explained to her that I was unsure how to tell her and that I felt it was better to leave her out of the whole situation. I assured her that I had always intended to come back and that I had never planned under any circumstances to stay in Oregon or to do anything to jeopardize our relationship. She was still a little confused, but happy nonetheless that I was back. I was glad to be back. I was growing even more fond of Brenda. Was I starting to fall in love with her?

June 2000 turned out to be an amazing time for me. I was now 20 years old. One day started out as a normal day for me, like every other day. The sun was out, there was a light breeze, and I felt relaxed and calm. Life was good. I had my girlfriend Brenda, a good job at the security company, and close friends I could turn to if necessary for support.

I went to work that night as usual at the apartment complex where I was living. It was a normal night, nothing out of the ordinary, just a few loud noise complaints that I had to deal with, or the occasional car speeding through the parking lot. Everything was business as usual. Then I started to feel funny. Something just did not feel right. I was still dealing with my hydrocephalus and epilepsy. Doctors had told me I'd have these conditions for the rest of my life and that I'd possibly have to have more surgeries to replace the shunt that controlled my hydrocephalus as I got older.

Suddenly I got a strange feeling in the right side of my neck where my shunt was. I immediately felt it to see if I could detect any problem with it. Whenever I had pain on that side it was a natural reaction to check the shunt, as my neurologist had shown me how to do. I pressed the valve just under my skin to see if it was filling up with fluids as it should. It wasn't. I started to worry. I continued to feel the shunt and noticed that it seemed to be broken apart in my neck, under the skin.

I immediately called my supervisor and told him I needed to go to the hospital. He understood and a friend drove me to the hospital in Turlock right away. I was taken to the emergency room, where an X-ray was performed. My hunch was correct. The shunt in fact had split apart in several places. I was then taken by ambulance to a hospital in Modesto, where a neurosurgeon was on duty. No neurosurgeon had been available at the hospital in Turlock.

When I arrived I was admitted immediately, then hooked up to a number of IVs. The next day the neurosurgeon told me that the CT scan they had performed the night before didn't show any immediate need for surgery. He said there was a possibility the shunt had not split apart and that it may just have been hiding behind muscle or something. I thought that what he was telling me made no sense.

He thought that since he was a doctor I should just believe whatever he told me. He tested the small pump located at the base of my neck just under my skin. (The pump was a one way valve that he could press in order to feel if fluid was filling up and draining correctly. It was much like pressing the pump on a lawn mower to prime the gas tank before starting it.) The pump filled. He said I must have pressed the wrong area when I'd begun to get worried. He told me to follow up with him in a week. We would decide then what the best course of action would be. I was released later that night. I left with many unanswered worrisome questions. I wondered what was really going on.

A week later I went back for the follow-up exam as directed, but when I got to the doctor's office it was closed. I could have sworn he had told me to come on Friday. I decided to go home and give him a call to set up another appointment. I was still having headaches and occasional pain on the right side of my head and neck. I was not sure what was causing all this. I took a couple of Tylenol, but they did not stop the pain. I tried to avoid focusing on it until I could get some answers at my follow-up appointment.

About a week or so later I returned to the Modesto hospital's emergency room with a high fever and redness along the site of my shunt. The doctors measured a 103.4 degree fever and said it was likely I had an infection caused by the shunt. (This is common with shunts and one of the reasons so many children and teens have shunt replacements.) I was admitted to the hospital again and put on strong antibiotics right away. The same neurosurgeon came in, examined me, now said he was sure the shunt had broken apart, and told me that they'd need to operate on me to fix it. Maybe he'd consulted with other doctors after I'd left the hospital the first time, since now he had a different opinion.

I thought it was about time they figured something out. Now they could do something to fix me. But I was also fearful. Even though I'd undergone four surgeries before, they all were done when I was little. It had been a long time since I'd been operated on. The last operation I'd had was when I was four, sixteen years earlier.

The surgery was scheduled for the next day. Brenda was in San Francisco driving her mother to the airport but she said she'd be back in Modesto in time for my surgery the next day. However, when the doctor came back in, he told me they'd be operating on me that night and not the next day. I got very anxious because I wanted Brenda to be there. She couldn't be, and there wasn't a thing I could do about it.

I wanted my parents to be there too, but we hadn't been in touch much since I'd moved to Turlock. I still felt they were disappointed that Nicole and I didn't get married and that I didn't stay with my son. And I still held a grudge against them for not wanting me to come home to live with them after I'd left Victor five years earlier. So I lay there in bed, alone, with no family or friends by my side. I was unsure how the surgery would go and was petrified at the thought that I might not wake up from it. I could die there that night. I could die there absolutely and totally alone.

About two hours later the doctor came in, shaved the back of my head, and explained the procedure to me. I was already somewhat familiar with it, as I'd had so many of these same surgeries as a child. I still remembered some things about the last operation I'd had at age four as if it were yesterday

I was wheeled into the operating room, hooked up to monitors, then told to count backwards from 100. I think I only got to 96. I awoke in a recovery room and was very groggy and disoriented. I felt my head and all I could feel was a massive bandage that seemed to cover almost my whole head. Only my face wasn't bandaged. I soon fell back to sleep.

I was informed later that Brenda had arrived just as I was wheeled to my hospital room from the recovery room. She stayed with me all night that night. The surgeon came to talk to me the next day, when I was a little more alert. I slept a lot off and on. I was pretty heavily medicated so pain was not a problem. I felt moderately dizzy and had a mild upset stomach. He said everything had gone well and that he had some good news for me.

I was not prepared for what he was about to say. He said I no longer needed the shunt and that the hydrocephalus was nonexistent! I could not believe what I'd just heard. I wondered what he was talking about. I asked him to repeat what he'd just said. He smiled and told me again. Again, I could not believe it. All my life I'd been told I'd need a shunt for the rest of my life. All my life I'd been told I might develop further complications and that I might need even more surgeries. All that went out the window when I heard what he'd said. This news was not what I'd expected. I asked him why. He just said that I'd outgrown the condition and that everything was fine. I was ecstatic.

My whole life I'd wished for something like this to happen and now my wish had actually come true. But why me? Why was I lucky enough to suddenly not have hydrocephalus anymore? The surgeon told me that I still had two catheters in my brain which could not be removed because brain tissue had grown around them. Also the risk of serious bleeding was too high if they tried to remove them. I was assured that having the catheters remain in my brain would not pose any problem at all. I was also told that scar tissue had formed around the path of the shunt tube under my skin. So even though the tubing itself had been removed, the path where the tubing had been would still be visible. Still, I was in disbelief.

I was informed that I'd have to stay in the hospital for a few more days in order to recover. I just could not believe that most of the shunt was now gone and the hydrocephalus that necessitated it was gone too. Just then I felt like the luckiest man alive.

One night while I was in the hospital and spaced out after being given big doses of painkillers, I started to miss Brenda very much. I unhooked all of the leads from the monitors, pulled the IV out of my arm, got dressed, and walked straight out of the hospital. I no longer had any head bandages. The doctor had taken them off a few days earlier so the incision would heal faster. You could see all the staples holding my incision closed. I was a real sight to behold.

I walked across the street to the store and bought a pack of cigarettes. People in line were staring at me with shocked looks on their faces. I was still on morphine and did not realize what they were staring at. After I bought the cigarettes, I used the pay phone outside to call Brenda. She was of course shocked and thought I was kidding. However, after I promised her I was telling the truth, she came and picked me up. I guess the hospital called her later to find out where I was. The next thing I knew I was back in my hospital bed. The doctor didn't come for two days after that. Maybe he was mad I'd left. When he came I apologized to him. He warned me about the danger of what I'd done. I apologized again, we shook hands, and that was that.

In September 2001 my precious daughter Anna was born. Talk about a proud papa! She was so small, delicate, and beautiful. She looked just like her mommy Brenda. As soon as she was born I told everyone I knew about her. I was so happy. She was as healthy as could be. I now had the same good feeling I'd had when my son was born two years earlier — the feeling of overwhelming joy and happiness that only having a child and becoming a parent can bring.

I looked at Anna with such amazement and vowed right then and there that I'd never give her up for anything. I'd protect her from any harm imaginable and would always put her needs first. I had been given a second chance to be a father and I was going to embrace that to the fullest. I went to work that night at the security company with great joy in my heart. Now I had an even greater reason to live and to make something of my life. Life, now more than ever, had a renewed purpose and meaning.

I still had not married Brenda. I wanted to make sure, now that we had a child together, that I was the man and father she wanted me to be. I wanted to show her that I could be a good provider and a good husband. I wanted to show her that, no matter what, I was willing to get up at night and tend to our daughter. I wanted Brenda to see me for the man I had become and would continue to be when we got married.

But, at the same time, I was still leery. The last time I'd become a father the woman I loved ran off with my son and never came back. I wanted to make sure that Brenda would have no reason in the world to ever want to do that.

15   Meeting my real father

The security company I worked for provided security for stores, warehouses, theaters, hotels, motels and apartment buildings. One night, while working security for a motel in Modesto, I started talking to a couple who I frequently saw standing just outside their room. They were a really friendly couple who always asked me how I was doing. They even brought out food for me from their room at times. They were staying at the motel as part of a program to house the homeless. The woman was black and very skinny. I thought she must be on drugs because of how skinny she was. Also, when she talked, she always slurred her words. Half the time her words did not make sense.

The man was white, about 6 feet 3 inches tall. He was almost bald, with just a few white hairs on the top of his head. He had no hair on his arms or face, not even any eyebrows or eyelashes. He also had problems talking. I could understand what he was saying, but I could also tell he was having a hard time pronouncing the words. Nevertheless, he was very kind and I really enjoyed talking to them both. I gave them a postcard from the motel to put in a scrapbook they were making and they were very appreciative.

I talked to them quite often over the two weeks I'd seen them there. One evening the woman made a comment that she was proud to be married to a Romine. I looked at her and asked her what she had just said. She repeated what she'd said. I told her that my biological father's last name was Romine. I knew there were quite a few Romines living in and around the area. I'd even phoned a few of them over the years to see if I could find any relatives, but I hadn't turned up any. The purpose of the calls was to see if some day I might be able to find my biological father, but I'd had no luck at all locating him.

Jackie, the woman, smiled, turned to the man and said, "Jerry, this may be the son you've been looking for all these years." What were the odds this man could be my biological father, the father I'd never known? What were the odds that this lucky break could happen to anyone? Surely this was not real. You only hear things like this happening on TV shows or in the movies. I thought when Jackie said that, that she must be drunk or high on something. From what my biological mother Leanne had told me, my biological father was either in jail or dead. Surely there was no way I would just happen to meet him in a chance encounter while at work twenty-one years later.

My heart must have skipped a beat. I'd never known anything about my biological father or even seen a picture of him. As far as I knew, from what Leanne had told me, he'd just picked up and left her before I was born. But I did know that his first name was Jerry. The man looked at me for a minute, then asked me if my mother's name was Leanne. I said, "Yes," and I backed up just a little. My heart started to beat just a little faster. Then he showed me a tattoo of a name inked on his right forearm. It was my mother's name, Leanne. I thought it must just be a coincidence.

I looked at him again. Then he said my two sisters' names. He even knew about the surgeries I'd had as a child. I could hardly believe what was happening. It was true. This man was the biological father I'd never known. We both must have thought the same thing at the same time. We embraced each other tightly and we both started to cry a little. I never thought I'd ever meet him, and now, out of the blue, against all odds, I'd run into him while working security at a motel. I felt like I'd just won the lottery.

I called Brenda and gave her the news. She started to cry and then came right away to see me at work. I announced over the security company radio to everyone working that night what had happened. Everyone started to reply with cheers and congratulations. I was just astounded. I promised Jerry I'd come see him the next day. He promised he'd take me to meet other family members I'd never known.

The next day I couldn't wait to go see my biological father. I now had my driver's license. Since having the shunt taken out, my epileptic seizures had completely stopped. I drove my car to pick up my father and we headed to another house. The house turned out to be very close to where I'd been living with Brenda, Anna and Brenda's mother. We went inside where I was introduced to Jerry Romine's mother, my grandmother Laverne.

There was another person there too, my brother Chris. I had no idea I had another brother. I knew my biological mother had had an older son named John, but he was the only brother I knew about. Jerry Romine's son Chris had a different mother, so I was his half-brother. This was amazing. I was so happy I could hardly contain myself. I hugged everyone. There was so much joy in that house that day.

I stayed for a while and ate lunch with them. We talked and talked and talked. My grandmother told me that my father had tried to be a part of my young life but that Leanne would not let him see me. Then she told me that later Leanne skipped town for parts unknown and took Julia and me with her. I knew nothing about this because Leanne had always told me that my dad had left her before I was born.

Then they showed me my baby pictures. They even gave me my baby book with all my pictures, birth information, clothes I wore, and ID tags I had on my feet just after birth. It was absolutely amazing! Laverne had kept all these things all these years. I was also told that I had an older half-sister named Tammy, who lived in Texas. I thought, "Wow! What else could I expect?"

There was so much to take in that I did not know what to make of it all. It was truly a shock. I left later that day, promising I would definitely come back to visit them often. After all, we still had so much to catch up on. Twenty-one years to be exact. I went back almost every day to Laverne's to visit. Every day something new happened. I met aunts and cousins I'd never known about. I learned about my family history, where my roots came from. I learned that I'd been named Jessie Fields Romine after my late grandfather, Laverne's husband, Bullett Fields Romine. He was a full-blooded Cherokee Indian. The story they told me was that, when he was born, he came out so fast that they named him Bullett. He was also born in a field, so he'd been given the middle name Fields. There were so many stories. I had no idea if they were all true.

Meeting my biological father really changed my perception of my entire life. I thought back to the time, as a young child, my biological mother was always telling me Jerry was either in prison or dead. I remember her telling me he had skipped town before I was born and that he wanted nothing to do with me. One of the reasons I'd always felt such intense anger and frustration was because I wanted to find him. I wanted to know him. And I wanted him to care about me. But I'd never been able to even locate any other relatives. I had needlessly harbored what felt was rejection by him for twenty-one years.

That night I finally realized that he had always loved me. I realized too that he had always wanted me. The way he hugged me and cried as he hugged me proved to me that he cared. I also learned that he had always tried to find me. I now believed with all my heart that he had never abandoned me. He had always wondered where I was and what my life was like. He even told me that he'd always wondered if he'd ever see me in his lifetime.

He could have refused to talk to me that night at the motel once he found out who I was. He could have easily just gone back into his room and shut the door and I would have gone on my way. But he didn't, so I believed him. I kept in contact with my new found family and made frequent trips to see them. I even called my half-sister Tammy in Texas and spoke to her. My new life was beginning to take shape.

16 Married ... with a mission

There was also something else that was burning inside me. I knew I did not have a college education. Every job I'd held had paid enough for me to pay my bills, but I wanted something more. Now that I had a daughter to raise, I needed something more. I felt that something was missing in my life. I thought maybe I could use what I'd learned from going through everything I'd gone through in life to help other people.

I was nowhere near perfect by any means, but I'd learned a lot. I'd lived through so much trauma. I'd made it through so many battles and defied so many odds that had seemed insurmountable at times. I'd also lived through and experienced miracles like my son and daughter being born. I'd made it through tough times living in a group home. I'd also experienced joy, which included not having hydrocephalus anymore and meeting my biological father for the first time.

Brenda and I were married in June 2003. She finally made an honest man out of me. The wedding was absolutely perfect. We had a large ceremony and reception in a beautiful garden in Turlock. I will never forget Brenda pulling up to the wedding garden in a vintage Rolls Royce. I could not hold back my tears. All I could think of was that this beautiful woman had stood by me through thick and thin, through so many of the bad things I'd gone through. She was a strong person, someone who wouldn't take no for an answer, and she loved and supported me. They say that opposites attract, and in our case, that's completely true.

My parents Jerry and Suzanne came to the wedding as well as my biological mother Leanne. I'd invited my biological father Jerry Romine and his family too. They said they'd come, but they didn't show up. I was hurt by that, but I knew that I'd just recently met them and that they were probably getting used to me, just as I was getting used to them. Julia's parents, Anne and Gary, came, as well as Jessica and her parents Judy and Ron. I'd invited Julia too, but she told me she couldn't come because she had to work.

The wedding celebration was everything I'd imagined it would be, everything I'd hoped for. All in all it was a wonderful day packed full of memories to last a lifetime. My daughter Anna, then a year-and-a-half old, was the flower girl. She looked precious in her special dress as she walked down the aisle. She looked just like her mama! Brenda and I danced into the wee hours of the morning. For once my life felt complete. It was a perfect night. I was finally perfectly happy.

Jerry Romine, my biological father, passed away in 2005. I was glad that at least I was able to meet the man who had helped make me. And I was happy to learn that he'd always loved me and had always wanted me. I was glad I'd had the chance to see where my family roots stemmed from and that I had been able to meet other family members I hadn't even known existed. I miss him and always will.

I often wonder what my life would have been like if he had been in the picture when I was young. I'm sad when I think about that. I wonder if Leanne would have kept me if he had stayed with her. I wonder if I would have grown up to be the successful person I am today or if I would have become someone totally different. But I can't be selfish. I enjoyed the time I'd had with him and he will always hold a special place in my heart.

I strongly believe that everything happens for a reason. I no longer regret anything I've done or anything I didn't do. I am the person I am today because of everything I've gone through and overcome. If anything in the past had been different, I might not be the person I am today. Sometimes I feel lucky that I had the past I had because it led to a calling, a real mission in life for me. At other times I just wish I'd had a simple, happy, normal beginning.

As I've described, I experienced a rough early childhood, and, as a result, I developed some serious mental health issues. In spite of this, I was able to turn my negative history into a positive life, a life in which I am able to grow, to succeed, and to help other people. I could have continued to dwell on the past and never move forward. But I chose to come to terms with it and use what I learned and experienced to make a positive change in the world.

One day I was looking in the newspaper and noticed an employment ad. It was for a position as a part-time youth counselor in a group home in Modesto. I applied and was accepted. Within a month of starting work there I was promoted to swing shift manager. To me this was not just a job. It was more of a calling. Because I'd lived in a group home and the experience had changed my life for the better, I understood the kids there. I could relate well to them and they respected me for that. It was a perfect fit. This was the purpose I'd been looking for in my life for many years. I had finally found it.

My duties consisted of making sure the kids were always safe and checking to see that they took their medications. I planned activities for them and took them regularly on trips to see movies, go bowling, go swimming, and do many other things they'd enjoy. But most of all, I was there to listen to their concerns. I was there to provide them understanding, support, and encouragement. I was their voice when they felt they did not have one. I could advocate for them when they could not.

Whenever the kids came to me to share stories about their past, I could understand them. Whenever they needed someone to talk to they could trust, I was available. I did not see them as problem kids who society had given up on. I did not see the negative futures that were in store for them if they continued on their destructive paths. Instead, I saw the positive things these kids could accomplish. I worked with 12 to 18 year old boys. Each came from similar neglectful and abusive backgrounds. Each came with his own history of pent up anger. Each came with his life turned upside down. It was my job to help each of them see the positive side of life.

Kids came and left the group home where I worked. Some completed the program and went home. Others couldn't adhere to the program's rules so they were sent to another program. A few even contacted me after they graduated from the program and thanked me for helping them, thanked me for making a difference in their lives. To me that appreciation was worth more than any amount of money in the world. I'd finally found my true calling — to help kids who were going through what I'd gone through.

Like a cat with nine lives, I'd survived my heart stopping at birth, five brain surgeries, a myriad of other physical and psychological problems, and two serious suicide attempts. I'd also survived Reactive Attachment Disorder. Yes, I was a survivor.

Afterword

As I fast forward to the present, I still work with teenaged boys in group homes. I respect them and they respect me. I don't think of my work as just a job. It is my passion and I think of it as my life's mission.

We all undergo trials and hardships in life. Whether or not we choose to use them as a crutch is solely up to us. In my case, I finally realized I could use what I'd learned from my tormented past as a powerful tool to help others succeed and prosper.

I am now the proud and happy father of three perfect little girls. At least they are perfect to me. I'm still married to Brenda. Although our marriage has had its trials and tribulations, we are happy together, and we make it work.

I've also changed my outlook on my adoptive parents, Jerry and Suzanne. For a long time I held grudges against them because I thought they'd given up on me. I thought that was why they'd taken me to the children's shelter when I was thirteen. I realized as an adult that I'd been wrong. They were determined for me to succeed in life and they knew that in order for that to happen I'd have to work through my severe emotional problems. They did the research necessary to realize that I had RAD. Most importantly, they already saw me as a suicide risk at age 13 and wanted to make sure I didn't die.

I'll be forever grateful to them and to my social worker Hale for making the tough but necessary decision to take me to the children's shelter so I could start getting the intensive help I needed. Perhaps the toughest decision a parent can make is to send their child away in order to get critical, even lifesaving, help. It can often be the best possible choice, especially when the decision is made out of love for the child.

I wanted to have a better relationship with my adoptive mom and dad. I wanted my kids to know what wonderful grandparents they have. I wanted them to be a part of my family again. We talk on the phone frequently now, and we have great conversations. They are a huge inspiration to me. I appreciate them now more than ever before. I love them with all my heart. At times I wish I could go back and change the way I'd been, but then I realize again that everything happens for a reason. I smile and move on.

My biological mother Leanne calls every now and then. She's still an alcoholic. Most of the time she's drunk when she calls, but it's still nice to hear her voice. I also now realize that she didn't give me up for adoption because she didn't want me. She gave me up so I'd have a chance at a better life. For that I love her and thank her. No matter what she did or will do in the future, she will always be the mother who gave me life. She will always be the one who allowed me to share my story today.

As an adult I still see the vestiges of RAD in me from time to time. I suspect I'll never completely overcome it, but I've come a very long way from where I began. I can proudly say that I survived it. I still occasionally have difficulty controlling my anger and showing my emotions. On rare occasions I struggle with trust issues, with closeness, with intimacy, with sharing my feelings, and with expressing love. I still have difficulty making eye contact with some people. I have trouble sometimes knowing when I need to let an argument go. These events are rare however, and my life is happy.

I have surrounded myself with very supportive people to help guide me along the way. My wife has been extraordinarily patient and compassionate. My adoptive parents have been there every step of the way, even when I did not realize they were. They continue to point me in the right direction and to give me all the necessary nudges along the way.

But the most important people in my life, beside Brenda, are my three young daughters. The minute I held my oldest daughter, just after she was born, I was a changed man. The minute she said, "Daddy," my heart melted. There is nothing I would not do for my little girls. I have vowed to raise them to have respect, dignity, and confidence and to feel secure and loved. I have vowed to break the cycle of abuse and neglect and I have done that. I promised myself and Brenda that our kids would never have to go through any unnecessary pain, suffering or fear. I often wonder what their lives are going to be like and what they'll grow up to be. But for now, they are my baby girls and they are living their childhoods the way that they should — happy and safe.

They give me the most contentment I have ever known. I hold them close to me every day. I caress them. I thank them for being my daughters. And I tell them they are the most important people in my life. I now know with absolute certainty that I'm no longer detached.

Practical suggestions for helping Reactive Attachment Disordered kids

On the following pages are some ideas, methods and techniques that may help your child overcome Reactive Attachment Disorder (RAD). They may also help your child's caregivers deal more easily with situations that may arise. I cannot guarantee that every suggestion will work for everyone, since every child with the condition is different. Many of these ideas worked well for me. Others worked for RAD kids I worked with. You will have to choose those best suited to your child's specific circumstances. But I can tell you that with knowledge, courage, will, perseverance, and hard work, RAD can be overcome.

Remember, neither the publisher nor I am a professional therapist or a practitioner of any sort. The following suggestions are offered without any guarantee of their efficacy. If you or your child is having difficulty coping, and anyone's safety is compromised, be sure to seek the assistance of a qualified professional.

The suggestions that appear on the following pages are just reflections, thoughts and ideas that have worked in my life and have worked for the teen boys I work with on a daily basis. Unless you have lived through and experienced RAD first hand, it is very hard to understand, let alone fully appreciate, what families go through every day.

Note that where I use the word "he" I intend it to mean "he or she." Where I use the word "child," the suggestions might work well for teens and adults too. I use the word "parent," but the suggestions are intended for anyone who works with RAD kids.

Caring for a RAD child is often a full-time job. Hopefully many of my suggestions will work for you. The sooner you put them into practice, the sooner your child will succeed.

SAFETY

1. Safety First! I can't stress this enough. Many kids with RAD only know anger and abuse, and are most likely to lash out when they are upset. Even if it's only to get attention, sometimes the child will go too far and end up seriously hurting himself or someone else. If, at any point, your child exhibits unsafe behaviors such as serious property damage, threatening you or other family members, harming himself by cutting himself, head banging, or other harmful actions, then you must seek help from a professional and/or call the authorities immediately.

2. When a child is loud and talks a lot, he is probably OK. When he's quiet and shut off, it's time to worry.

ADOPTED RAD KIDS

3. Many RAD kids are adopted. Do not knowingly adopt a RAD child if your life isn't already filled with love. You won't get the love you're seeking from a child unable to give it, at least for a very long time.

WAITING FOR MATURITY

4. Just waiting for a RAD child to grow up and mature isn't the answer. He will not just "outgrow" the condition.

MAKE DECISIONS NOW

5. Give the most attention to finding solutions to the most extreme behavioral problems first.

6. Do whatever you need to do to get help for your child, even if everyone you know criticizes you or even tells you you're a bad parent.

7. If you realize you've done everything possible to help your child and you're unable to make a difference, investigate and follow up on every resource, every lead you can find.

8. If you know something will need to be done sooner or later, just bite the bullet and do it now.

HOPE AND THE FUTURE

9. Make a large poster with two columns. Write "I can do nothing about" in big letters atop the left column. Write "I can do everything about" in big letters atop the right column. Then assist your child in filling in the blank spaces in each column.

10. You can't walk forward if you're looking backward. Keep helping your RAD child concentrate on the now and the near future. Keep reminding him he can do absolutely nothing about the past. Keep telling him he can do everything about the present and future though.

11. Tell him that taking responsibility for his actions makes him really powerful. After all, if he can create problems, then he can also create solutions. His choices determine success or failure. Blaming someone else for his problems saps his power because he has little or no control over other people. Tell him he can have a terrific future but that it's all up to him.

12. Drive him around to see the nicest house in the nicest neighborhood. Tell him when he's older, if he works hard, he could be living in that house, in that neighborhood, and enjoying a good life. Tell him you can picture him grown up and living there surrounded by his own happy family.

13. For an older child, tell him about different kinds of jobs or professions out there that might interest him. See if something sparks his interest that you can help him pursue.

14. You have to remain hopeful that he will change for the better, that he'll have a bright future, and that eventually he'll want to include you in his life.

EMPTY SHELLS

15. Many RAD kids are "empty shells" just waiting to be filled. Some have suffered severe deprivation. Sometimes you can "fill them up" a little at a time with simple things like telling them they can play with any toy in the room, catch as many fish as they want, eat as many of their favorite snacks as they want, have as many coloring books as they want, etc. Give a child one of these experiences every week or two. What can they have an unlimited supply of?

REWARDS

16. Reward even the smallest signs of good behavior or progress with an immediate verbal comment like "good job" or "well done" and a pat on the back.

17. Give constant verbal praise for positive behavior.

18. Even if your child is cussing on the way to a time out, praise him for at least going to the time out location and for following directions. Baby steps first.

19. Use immediate rewards, as most RAD kids can't see very far into the future. They can only focus on having their immediate needs met. For example, post a 'success chart' in the house. Put the child's name in big letters at the top. List the tasks the child needs to complete that day, like reading a chapter in a book, tying his shoes properly, doing

his math homework, etc. For each completed task, put a big red star next to the task when the child successfully completes it. At the end of the day, when the chart is filled with red stars, give the child an immediate reward. Do this every day.

20. Tell your child that you love him all the time. Even though love alone will never be enough to "cure" a RAD child, instilling in his mind every day that he is loved, will, over time, let him realize that someone does care for him. Keep telling him this even when you don't get any response back and even if it seems he isn't listening. He probably is.

21. Don't belittle or make fun of your child. It's easy for us to get extremely frustrated and say things we cannot take back.

IGNORE THE NEGATIVE, EMPHASIZE THE POSITIVE

22. Unless the child's behavior is dangerous, ignore negative behavior. This will stop him from exhibiting negative behavior in order to get attention.

23. Make certain your child learns how to ignore and avoid any negative influences and bad people around him so he can just focus on his own issues. Avoid distractions. Self-focus.

24. After his bad behavior is finished, talk to the child about why the behavior was exhibited and what he could do differently next time.

25. Show your child better alternatives for the behavior he's exhibiting.

26. Provide the opportunity for daily activities with positive interactions, such as playing board games together, going on picnics or outings, or doing some physical activity together.

27. Do relaxing family things like fishing, camping, canoeing, singing, joking, storytelling, walking, and hiking as often as your schedule permits.

28. Smile and laugh with your child. Smiling is very healthy. Life can be fun. Life is full of opportunities. When we smile and laugh we feel happier, healthier, and people want to be around us. When we're mad and upset all the time, no one really wants to be around that. Not having positive people around us can lead to more depression, which hurts our bodies and minds.

29. Seek out comedies on TV, DVDs and at the movies. Laughter alleviates stress and is clearly good for both body and soul.

30. Have your child join the Cub Scouts or similar organizations that build character and give awards for achievement.

31. On a large piece of paper write down positive words that describe your child and tape it to his bathroom mirror so he can see those words every day when he looks in the mirror.

32. Don't let your child put himself down. The more he puts himself down, the more he will fail. Remind him, "You are a good person and there are good people out there to assist you in working through your issues and becoming successful. Be proud of who you are and who you can become. Be proud that you are trying to feel better. Be proud that you want to make a difference in the world, to do something good to help other people. Be proud of what you've overcome so far and the progress you are making! Always stay positive."

33. Don't let anyone tell your child that he can't achieve something. This is by far my favorite. So many people in my life were always putting me down because they didn't understand what I was going through or

the life that I'd had. It's very easy to look at someone and say they'll never amount to anything. Always know that whatever you and your child put your minds to, you can accomplish. Sure, it will take some hard work, but it takes less work to succeed than it does to fail. If you think it, then you can do it!

34. The only thing standing between success and failure are the choices you and he make together.

35. Don't give up hope. Just because you may not see immediate results doesn't mean there will never be results. Just because you're having a hard time now doesn't mean the future will be hard. If you and your child work hard, set goals, and listen to people trying to help you, positive things will happen. Although it may take a while, it is possible for your child to survive RAD and to have a happy, success- ful, prosperous life.

36. Start by focusing on getting him to learn to trust. Have him think about all the times that someone promised him something and followed through with that promise. Make a list of them if necessary.

37. Ask him to understand that even though you may disapprove of some, or even most, of his behavior, you still love him and want the best for him.

38. Say, "I love you" and follow it immediately with an "I love you" action.

39. Tell him he's a good person and he has a lot going for him.

40. Tell your child he is a very important person in your life. Thank him for being your child.

41. Promise your RAD child that he will improve. He may have to take the first step and take a leap of faith, but sooner or later he will feel better.

42. Stop the cycle of abuse and neglect. Have you ever heard the phrase "I was abused as a child so that is all I know"? This is an excuse. We all have the power to stop that cycle. Ask your child, "Is the life you're living now what you want? Do you want to continue to be angry? When one day you have a family of your own, do you want your family to experience what you have experienced?" Probably not. Breaking that cycle starts with him wanting to change his way of thinking.

43. Don't let your child dwell on the past. Holding on to any anger he feels doesn't help him or anyone else in his life. He can't change anything that happened in the past. It's already done. None of it can be taken back. He'll only get more upset and depressed, which doesn't help him heal. Try to encourage him to forgive and move on. While he may never forget what happened to him, he can over time decide to forgive. He will eventually, however slowly, be able to let go of the past.

44. Always ask, "Where's the evidence?" What facts back up your child's beliefs about what happened or is happening to him? Write these down, then examine the facts carefully.

45. Encourage your child to be willing to take "emotional risks." That means he needs to be willing to open up to people he trusts and he shares what he's feeling.

46. Don't make excuses for him or let him blame other people for his mistakes. Get him to take responsibility for his actions. No one wants to hear excuses. They want to hear what positive steps he's going to

take to work through his issues and succeed. It's OK for him to make mistakes as long as he learns from them and tries to avoid repeating them. Life does not come with an instruction manual, so most often we learn by trial and error and from our parents and others around us.

47. Find out who his friends are, even if you have to pry. Don't let him hang around the wrong crowd. Look for friends he can surround himself with who care about him and really understand him, rather than those who say they are friends only to take advantage of him. If he starts to associate with negative people, ones who behave badly, he may become even more negative and get into really serious trouble.

48. Don't get into a power struggle with your child. This is like candy to a RAD child, who longs for argument and for control. It's very easy to get hooked in, and when you do, you'll find it will become a losing, exhausting battle.

49. Pick your battles. Forget about all the minor things your child may be doing wrong.

CALM, LOW VOICE, EYE LEVEL

50. When listening to a RAD child it's important to sit, bend down, or kneel so you're at eye level with him.

51. Stress to the child that, while you understand why he feels the way he does, that does not excuse bad behavior.

52. Try to understand and empathize with him. Use active listening. Ask pointed questions which can help the child express how he's feeling.

53. Keep your composure. Don't let him rattle you, no matter what he says or does.

54. Read him calming, happy bedtime stories.

55. If your child is upset, allow 5 to 10 minutes for him to be alone. Then talk to him about what happened and offer solutions on how to handle the situation differently the next time.

56. Wait for the child to start to calm down. Don't yell at or threaten him. Many RAD kids come from a background of severe abuse or neglect. We don't want to add "more fuel to the fire." A loud angry voice fuels anger and by calming our voices we tend to start to breathe better. When we breathe better, we calm down too.

57. Don't let your anger and frustration get in the way of your goals. The sooner your child overcomes RAD, the sooner you'll all get more enjoyment out of life!

58. When your child raises his voice to you, lower your voice. Speak to him in a calm reassuring "your behavior doesn't phase me" tone of voice. He wants to hear what you are saying because he wants that attention. In order for him to hear you, he will have to lower his voice.

59. It helps immensely if you can recognize the things that trigger your child's bad behaviors. If you can stop something before it happens, you are one step ahead and everyone benefits.

HUGS AND KISSES
60. Ask your child if it's OK to hug, kiss or touch him before doing so.

61. If your child feels threatened by close physical contact, try blowing him a kiss.

62. Don't hug your child from behind or face-to-face, as this can be too frightening. Try hugging from the side so he feels he has a quick exit if he's uncomfortable.

63. Give a younger child lots of stuffed animals to hug.

SIMPLE FIVE WORD REQUESTS

64. When asking your child to do something, use no more than five words at a time (for example, "Jeff, please look at me.", "Justin, are you ready?", "Want to pick a story?", or "Could you set the table?"). The "rule of five words or less" allows the parent to give clear, concise instructions that are simple to follow.

65. When you're giving instructions, tell the child only one thing at a time. This allows one task to be completed at a time so it is easier for the child to understand.

66. Don't think that, just because you gave instructions, your child will know what to do. You have to give clear descriptions of what you want done and the time frame it has to be done in. And, as always, give praise for the follow through.

67. State your request in as few words as possible and leave it at that. If your child does not follow through, prompt once or twice. If he's still defiant, ignore the behavior. Soon he'll see that the attention is not there.

VOLUNTEERING

68. Volunteer with him to go help someone else. Even if you do this for just an hour a week, the child will see there are people out there in even worse straights than he is. He may also start to develop empathy or even a sense of purpose. Choose volunteer activities in which the

child will see direct immediate results of his efforts (for example, handing out food at a food bank).

CONSISTENCY, FOLLOW THROUGH

69. Consistency is extremely important. Be consistent with rules, structure, and consequences. The same good behavior must result in the same reward. Extreme negative behavior should result in the same negative consequences each time. The negative consequences should fit the negative behavior in severity and type. For example, if the child cuts holes in the shirt he's wearing, have him buy a new shirt with his allowance or have him repair the shirt by sewing the holes closed.

70. Both parents must be on the same page. If not, the RAD child will play one parent against the other. If you're alone and your child asks for something and you're not certain you're on the same page as your spouse, wait to answer until you can consult with him.

71. To build trust, tell the child the time frame in which you'll be completing whatever you promised him you'll do. Give yourself more than ample time so you can always do it within that time period.

72. Make sure you follow through on the limits you set. If you have to give consequences, then make sure they are the same each time the behavior presents itself.

73. Utilize your partner and any understanding friends and relatives if you're getting burned out. Having other people there to "relieve you" can provide a much needed break.

BE COGNIZANT OF HIS ACTIVITIES

74. RAD kids need constant attention and monitoring.

75. Be "in his face." Don't give your child the privacy that would provide him the time and space to do destructive things. Constantly ask him where he's going and what he's doing. Just say these things in a calm, non-threatening way.

76. Don't let him dodge questions or try to skip talking about sensitive issues. RAD kids put up defensive "walls" to hide their feelings. Your job is to break down those walls stone-by-stone or brick-by-brick in order to find out what's really going on.

77. Check in with him all the time. If he's home, you may want to ask him to leave the door to his room open. If he's away from home, find out where he is, what he's doing, and when he plans to be back home.

78. If he tells you he's going to visit friends, call their parents to verify that what your child has told you is true.

79. Trust, but verify. Sometimes, don't even trust.

80. Check in with his school teachers and counselors all the time.

81. Tell him how he can reach you at all times.

SET GOALS

82. Tell him you know he can succeed in reaching his goals.

83. Create and explain "behavior levels" for the child. When the child's at the lowest level, level one, he gets no privileges. When he goes up levels due to good behavior, he gets more and more privileges, a bigger allowance, etc. This method is very easy to implement and works really well.

84. The best and shortest route to achieving high self-esteem is through achievement, through mastering tasks given to us. Set goals for your child. Make realistic goals he can achieve. I set daily, weekly and monthly goals. Every time I reached those goals, it made me feel really good inside. It allowed me to see that I was succeeding and moving forward. Goals are always good in everyday life. Your child may have to be nudged a little (or a lot) to try hard to reach them. It does no good to set goals and then give up on them. Should you feel the goal you set is too hard, take a look at it and decide if you're at a point where your child can reach that goal. If not, then it's OK to rewrite it so he can achieve it. But don't make it too easy. He has to challenge himself and tirelessly forge ahead.

85. Set goals together with your child, goals that are attainable in a reasonably short amount of time. Goals are very important. They provide a good tool to keep you on track. They should be easy to understand and somewhat easy to achieve. Make daily goals such as "I will have a positive day and complete whatever tasks are assigned to me." He should also have weekly goals such as "In one week, I will have initiated a conversation with a close friend" or "In one week I will have attended school every day of the week and completed all assignments." Every goal is different and will vary according to each situation. There should also be monthly goals. This one is a little harder, as he has 30 days to finish this. Maybe the goal is learning to share how he's feeling, turning in a certain number of job applications, or maybe in the 30 days he'll have fewer than four anger outbursts. Whatever the goals are that you set with him, they should be designed by him, with your assistance, to help him work through his problems.

86. Write up contracts with your child which can result in him receiving immediate rewards, weekly rewards and monthly rewards. These work well. They allow the child to monitor his own progress and they provide a great tool to help motivate him. For example, if your child

is having difficulty and tends to act out every day when he doesn't get what he wants, then you could make a contract entitled "Acting Out." In that contract you could start off by stating what the issue is: "I (name of child) realize that every time I do not get my way, I start yelling, throwing things, and breaking objects. In order to help me improve in this area, I agree to comply with the following terms." Keep the terms easy to understand and achievable for the first week. This will show the child he can make progress. This will help him build self esteem.

You should have one main term and two sub-terms that relate to the main term. For example, "Term one: I agree that every time I do not get my way and I feel like acting out, I will not throw things. Term two: If I do not throw things when I am acting out, I will receive immediate verbal praise from my parents/caregiver. Term three: When I have calmed down after acting out, I will talk to my parents/care-giver about what made me upset and talk about what I could do differently next time."

Of course, this is just an example, and this may not be what behavior your child is exhibiting. The contract can be reworded as needed to fit your child's actions. Another important part of the contract is giving rewards for abiding by it. Keep in mind that he may not succeed at this 100% of the time and it's not fair to expect him to. A good start is usually 80%. If he doesn't abide by the contract but calms down and talks about what made him upset, that is a step in the right direction.

The reward should be simple and something he wants. It could be video game time, staying up late, or maybe a special treat. These are all good for daily rewards for abiding by the contract. Weekly rewards for doing really well should be something a little bigger like going out to dinner, or getting a special toy.

You should all sign the contract so everyone understands and is on the same page. This is very important. Don't forget to follow through with the rewards! Again, this is just an example of a contract that I use in my work and it has proven to be very effective. The contracts can be tailored to whatever your child's behavior is and whatever you would like to see changed.

Remember, focus on the small changes. Contracts are not designed for big changes to take place right away and it's very important that we recognize even the smallest positive changes and that we give verbal praise immediately! Contracts may not work for everyone. You may have already tried the reward contract system, star charting or other ideas. As we know, not every idea works for every child. But keep plugging away. Maybe something that didn't work six months ago will work now.

87. Teach him step-by-step how to succeed at tasks. Write down the steps for him using numbers 1, 2, 3, etc.

BOUNDARIES

88. Remember, you are not his friend. You are his parent, caregiver, social worker, etc. Giving in to what the child wants when you know it's bad for him is never a good thing. He does not have veto power over your decisions.

89. Set appropriate boundaries for your child and ask him what appropriate means to him. Emphasize that it's important to respect the child and adult boundaries. That goes both ways. That is, don't talk about adult things with kids, and kids should not expect to be involved with adult matters.

LET HIM DECIDE

90. Offer three or four possible choices in any given situation in which all choices are appropriate good ones. Let your child pick one of the solutions. This allows your child to have some control over the situation. For example, would he like to help unpack the groceries, set the table, or empty the dishwasher? Or would he like to read a few

chapters from his choice of books? Would he like to go fishing or hiking or swimming?

UNCOMFORTABLE PLACES

91. Don't send him on "time outs" to places where he'll feel isolated or punish him by sending him to his room. Most importantly, don't ever lock your child in a room unless he poses an immediate danger to someone in the house. Locking him in a room may make some matters worse because of the RAD child's feelings of abandonment and isolation. Give him time outs by asking him to sit in a chair and be quiet in a room you're in, unless the child likes going to his room.

92. Have "time-ins," where consequences for bad behavior include doing a chore with you he doesn't like to do.

ONE STEP AT A TIME

93. Have patience. Even if he makes the smallest positive change, that is progress. Take that progress and build on it. Good things will come. Just take one day at a time.

94. You cannot "fix" the problem overnight, or in a week, or even in a month. The child's problems took many years to build up. It will take quite a while for him to overcome them. Know that things can and will get better over time.

ENCOURAGE OPENNESS ABOUT FEELINGS

95. Remember that most acting out is for a deeper reason. See if you can find out what that reason is.

96. Teach your child the best words to express his emotions.

97. Tell him it's OK to cry and to feel sad.

98. If he ever tells you how he's feeling, repeat back to him what you heard him say. Say, "I heard you saying ...... ," then say, "I understand."

99. Search for a school counselor or another adult the child feels comfortable confiding in. Encourage him to talk freely in private with that person. Understand that if he doesn't choose you as the person he feels most comfortable confiding in, that's normal. Don't take it personally.

100. Be compassionate. Understand that everyone feels pain and love and joy and everyone has a different way of showing those emotions. Try to listen and understand what he is going through.

CONSEQUENCES

101. Consequences versus punishment. Yes, there is a difference. A consequence is something that makes sense. Consequences are designed to help your child learn and change. Punishments are designed to strike fear and maintain control. Examples of consequences are things like going to bed earlier if he stayed up later than he should have, more study time for lower grades, toys taken away for misuse, game systems taken away for bad behavior. There are many more, but you get the idea. Punishments, however, are different. Being beaten, being belted, having food taken away, even being spanked are all examples of punishments. Empty threats are also never good. These do not work and in the long run they generate more fear and anxiety and do not solve anything.

102. It can be counter-productive if you give your child consequences while the bad behavior is still going on. This doesn't work because they are not in the right frame of mind to hear what you are saying. This can even agitate the situation. Once your child has calmed down and is in a better space, then talk about what happened and ask him what he thinks is a fair consequence for his behavior. This

should be a compromise so he can see that you are trying to work with him and not against him. Don't be afraid to disagree however if he thinks he doesn't deserve any consequences.

103. Consequences are not a bad thing. RAD kids do not have much of a concept of right and wrong. Consequences should be designed to help the child learn right from wrong and learn cause and effect. Of course we do not want to bury the child with so many consequences that he feels hopeless. Consequences may not work for all children. You have to find what works best in any given situation with your child.

ANGER RELEASE

104. Don't let him keep anger bottled up inside. This can be very dangerous. When we keep anger inside and don't have a positive outlet to release it, it festers and grows. We can only hold so much and when we try to fit more in, we explode! When we explode with our anger we can do bad things without realizing what we are doing. When we get older and have our own family, if we still are angry, this can lead to serious domestic violence.

105. Give him healthy ways to release anger, like showing him how to take his aggression out on a punching bag.

106. Letting him play rhythmic music and percussion instruments like a drum may also help.

107. Another anger release option is to take him somewhere out in the open, far from "civilization" and let him scream at the top of his lungs.

108. A younger child may be able to calm himself by running around in a safe area like a park.

109. Tiring him out usually calms him down too.

110. Teach him breathing techniques he can use to calm himself down when he's angry. Show him how to breathe in deeply through his nose, then exhale through his mouth. Concentrating only on breathing will clear his mind and let him regain self-control.

111. Teach an older child to take long walks to calm himself.

112. Count to ten before reacting. Teach your child to do the same. RAD kids have poor impulse control, so this is a good exercise for him.

TEACH SOCIAL GRACES

113. Teach him how to handle awkward social situations like meeting people for the first time, making friends on the playground, and what to say on the phone. Role play with him so he can practice with you how to act and what to say.

114. Teach him the qualities to look for in friends and those to avoid.

115. Teach him how to make eye contact by choosing someone he feels safe with and having him "practice" with that person.

116. Teach your child empathy. If he harms someone say, "How would you feel if someone did that to you?"

IGNORE HIS REJECTION

117. Trust comes before love can come. RAD kids have to learn how to love. But first they have to learn to trust. As you show them that no matter what they call you, no matter what they say to you, no matter how much they reject you, that you're still there, they will probably begin to open up a little. They need an outlet to express their anger

and if they can see that you can take it and not walk away, they will begin to feel more comfortable and at ease. Their respect level will rise and their behavior will start to change because they begin to see they can trust you.

118. Do everything you can to avoid taking any rejection by your child personally. Don't feel the child does not love you. He has a lot of anger and hurt and most often lashes out at the people closest to him. Most often he's testing you to see if you'll stick around after he puts you down, calls you names, lies, steals, manipulates you, and rejects any love and affection you give him.

119. When you try to show affection and your child pushes you away, it may be because he just isn't used to receiving affection and it's strange to him.

SCHOOL

120. Show him how learning in school is relevant to his life. For example, fractions learned in math class that day can be applied right away to a dinner recipe you're making. See if you can do this every day, if possible, with something he's learned that week in school.

121. Don't let your child drop out of school. School is very important. He must earn at least a high school diploma or G.E.D. He'll need this degree in order to get a decent job or perhaps go on to college. If he doesn't earn a diploma or G.E.D, his life will probably be very hard. If he drops out of school, his life may prove to be even harder than it is now.

   Staying in school will also give him less time to be alone. He will build friendships in school that can last a lifetime. If he's having trouble in school, make an appointment with his school counselor or a favorite teacher to discuss what's troubling him. They are great problem solvers and most of the time they can offer you ideas and help that you never knew were available.

JOURNAL/WRITING/DRAWING

122. Help your child search for the people he feels abandoned him or harmed him in other ways. When you find them, ask them about what happened until you get the answers you need. The risk here is that you may not find them, or you child will experience further rejection or stonewalling by them. Keep asking them questions. You both need the answers. If you feel there may be a face-to-face confrontation, be sure to bring someone with you who makes your child feel safe.

123. If you can't do this, another option is to have your child write letters to them, telling them exactly how he feels and how their actions affected him. Have him write all the questions down he can think of.

124. Get a piece of paper and a pencil or pen. Ask your child to start writing down everything that is on his mind — feelings, concerns, anxieties, frustrations, things that make him happy, things that make him sad, his goals, his dreams and more. You'll find that as he starts to write, these feelings will start to be released from his mind and be put onto paper. He should feel better every time he does this.

125. Have him keep a personal journal, where he can write or draw anything he wants. This allows for ideas in his head to be transferred to paper. Writing or drawing these thoughts helps the child get rid of his "emotional baggage."

126. If he's too shy to talk to anyone about how he feels, have him show people a page or two from his journal.

127. Or, if you prefer, have him keep a diary by his bed that he can write in every night. Many people have a hard time falling asleep because, while they're resting, their mind is spinning so fast with thoughts. Writing in his journal before going to bed should help him sleep better.

128. If he likes to draw more than he likes to write, have him draw pictures of how he's feeling. Have him show these to anyone he feels comfortable showing them to.

129. Have him write down every day three things he's thankful for. This is all very useful and does work!

130. It can also be helpful to have him write a thank you letter to someone once a week.

DAILY/WEEKLY CALENDAR

131. Another tool that I've found to be very useful and that was very effective in helping me was being able to see a posted schedule of the daily or weekly events. This allowed me to see what was going to happen every day so I could be less anxious. I was always fearful of the unknown and having a posted schedule of activities lessened my fears and made me feel more in control.

132. Allow the RAD child to participate in planning the daily and weekly schedules, including meal planning.

LEARN ABOUT RAD

133. Read and understand everything you can about your child's condition so you can have a better idea why he does some of the things he does. This also helps you see that you are not alone as a RAD parent/caregiver and that many other parents/caregivers are going through or have gone through the same thing. Besides

searching in libraries and bookstores, check online for any reliable information on RAD, and join one or more Facebook groups or blogs centered around RAD.

FOOD

134. Don't use food as a punishment. For example, don't feed other children in your house one thing and feed your RAD child something different as a punishment. Lack of food could be an issue these kids have had to face in the past. They may have come from very poor households where food was scarce and they did not know where their next meal was coming from.

135. Personally serve the child his food.

136. If a child is hungry, offer fruit, which should be available all the time. It's healthy and can offer a much needed snack between meals.

SLEEP

137. Make sure your child is getting enough sleep. Sleep deprivation is a serious factor in depression, so it makes RAD worse.

VALIDATION

138. Tell him not to feel he always has to be right. No one is right all the time. It's OK to listen to other people and try their ideas. It's OK to be wrong at times. This is how we learn and this is how we grow. If we were right all the time, then how would we mature and grow? The world would be a very boring place, with nothing to learn.

139. Don't over-parent by saying things like, "When I was a child, I was made to do this........" Few of us have experienced what your child with RAD has gone through. When you bring up your past, your child may feel that his current life is not important to you. Validation is very important to him.

DISCOMFORT/FEAR

140. Don't force a child to do anything that he's very fearful of. This will only back him into a corner and start a new cycle of anger and regression. These kids have to learn at their own pace. While they have to be held accountable, not every child is going to learn like the next. They have to learn to trust. They have to learn to crawl before they can learn to walk. Give them positive reasons why they should try doing the task you're about to give them. If necessary, support their decision to back off from the task, but later offer them more chances to finish it so they can feel more at ease doing it.

SUPPORT

141. Don't assume every psychiatrist and psychologist can correctly diagnose or effectively treat RAD. Excellent practitioners are out there. Keep looking until you find one. Part of your search should include asking them interview questions about RAD that you already know the answers to. See what they know about the condition and how to treat it.

142. Look for a support group of people going through similar situations. If you don't find one, start one. With a support system you'll be able to talk to other parents/caregivers who understand your situation and who can help guide you along the way.

143. If your child feels no one is listening to him, keep searching for someone who will. What about his teachers, school counselors, coaches, friends, his friends' parents, relatives, neighbors, your minister, people at church, people at any organization you belong to, his doctors? The more good listeners you find the better, even if you're a good listener.

RESIDENTIAL TREATMENT OPTIONS

144. Understand that the toughest decisions can be the best decisions. Deciding to send your child to a residential treatment facility, for example, can be a very tough decision to make. You will miss him. You may feel you are giving up on him. You may feel that he will be angry with you, that he won't trust you anymore, and that he may feel you've betrayed him. But I can tell you from personal experience, in the long run, your child will get the much needed therapy he needs in order to become the loving, caring, mature person you want him to be.

Many parents may make the decision to place a child in residential care because they feel guilty for giving up on their child. They feel like a bad parent and that they are contributing to the child's abandonment issues. But the other side is, if you don't take immediate action, the outcome can be far worse. You are not a bad parent. In fact, making the call shows that you love your child and care for his well being as well as the safety of everyone in your household. You have to do whatever is necessary to protect the child from self harm, and to protect the rest of your family from harm. Sometimes you may even need to send him to a treatment facility far from home, or separate him from others in your home to keep them out of danger.

How to contact the author

Jessie Hogsett can be reached at:

e-mail   Jhogsett80@yahoo.com

blog   radjhogsett.blogspot.com

Your comments and feedback are appreciated!

CPSIA information can be obtained
at www.ICGtesting.com
Printed in the USA
FFOW01n1749110416
23181FF